THE NAKED ARTIST
COMIC BOOK LEGENDS

by BRYAN TALBOT

with illustrations by
HUNT EMERSON

First MOONSTONE edition 2007

THE NAKED ARTIST:
Comic Book Legends

ISBN 10 digit: 1-933076-25-9   13 digit: 978-1-933076-25-6

Cover Illustration by Hunt Emerson

Book Design and Prepress by
Erik Enervold/Simian Brothers Creative

Interior Illustrations by Hunt Emerson

Printed in USA

PUBLISHER'S NOTE:

This is a work of fiction. Names, characters, places, and incidents either are the products of the authors' imagination or are used fictitiously, and any resemblance to actual persons, living or dead, business establishments, events, or locales is entirely coincidental.

Published by Moonstone, 582 Torrence Ave, Calumet City, IL 6040
www.moonstonebooks.com

To: Mathew

*A big tip of the hat to some of the folk from whom I've heard
these stories or who've provided relevant information:
Leo Baxendale, Norm Breyfogle, Kurt Busiek, Al Davison,
Jamie Delano, Hunt Emerson, Garth Ennis, Glenn Fabry,
Neil Gaiman, Dave Gibbons, Igor Goldkind, Archie Goodwin,
Alan Grant, Steven Grant, John Higgins, Bob Ingersoll,
Lovern Kindzierski, Todd Klein, Bill Knapp, Ilpo Koskela,
Dave Langford, Garry Leach, Tony Lee, Steve Leialoha,
Heidi MacDonald, John McCrea, John McShane, Frank Miller,
Gary Spencer Millidge, Leah Moore, Grant Morrison, Michael Netzer,
Lee Nordling, Frank Plowright, John Reppion, Eric Reynolds,
Trina Robbins, Will Simpson, Dez Skinn, Robert Sprenger,
Jim Steranko, Colin Upton, Rick Veitch, Lawrence Watt-Evans,
Shannon Wheeler, Marv Wolfman, Steve Yeowell*

*The rest are lost to my rapidly deteriorating memory,
purveyors of comic book legends all.*

*A great big sloppy thank you to novelist Chaz Brenchley for
test-driving the almost finished book and making road kill
of the vast majority of typos.*

*For those of a sensitive disposition and to those who are
easily offended, just bugger off.*

Illustrations by HUNT EMERSON

INTRODUCTION
PROS & CONS

The British satirical cartoonist Steve Bell, talking about his *Guardian* newspaper strips, once said that artists must live in a world of their own. And, for the most part, we do. For most comic creators, it's a pretty solitary existence. Working from home, we spend entire days in our own company, perhaps just seeing family or friends at night, lost in the lands of our own imagination. If there's an imminent deadline we'll work till the small hours of the morning or all night, if necessary. If I'm at home I work every day of the week till nine at night. It's all I can do to make it out of the house to the gym three times a week. That's the trouble with being self-employed. The boss is a total bastard.

Don't get me wrong: I'm not complaining. I love it. I love getting up at whatever the hell time I want to. After working at jobs in the distant past where I've had to travel an hour and a half to get there in the middle of winter at seven in the morning, I love being able to just walk downstairs to arrive at work. I love spending the whole day creating stories, surrounded by my books and junk, with no jumped-up muppet of a manager breathing down my neck. And, generally speaking, I love the comic business, the people and the events.

Perhaps it is because we spend all this time on our own that, when we do get out to conventions, some of us tend to let rip a little: drinking too much, staying up far too late chatting with colleagues whom we haven't seen for ages or ones that we've only just met, networking, news-gathering and telling stories, often stories about other pros at other conventions who've drunk too much and stayed up far too late. Incestuous? You bet.

Like the novice private dick who's trailing Phillip Marlowe in Raymond Chandler's *The Little Sister* who feels an affinity with Marlowe and happily supplies him with inside information because they're both "in the same racket", we seem to have this bond because we work in the same medium. We all know its characteristics, its grammar, its history and the people who populate the industry. Sometimes–rarely now but utterly transcendental when it happens–I'll be at a convention or comic festival in some foreign town and suddenly, out of the blue, I'll get an intoxicating rush simply from being part of this international community of comic creators, a sort of involuntary and unexpected tribal ecstasy. I can recognize it when I see it in the eyes of other creators when it hits them. It's easy to spot. They look like they've just had a spontaneous frontal lobotomy.

I'm not claiming that we all love each other like the sibling pinheads in Tod Browning's *Freaks*. In fact some pros hate each other's guts with a passion, usually through some past business or creative dispute, though often it's down to pure personality clash. In a very, very tiny percentage of cases it's because someone has a personality that's about as attractive as a giant incontinent zombie slug with a penchant for projectile vomiting. That's very rare. On the whole, comic people are sociable, funny and interesting and the industry is certainly a lot nicer business to be in than the movie and TV industry or the world of popular music, going by my limited experience.

But, yes, get us together and we'll talk about each other, whether to hear gossip, enquire about old colleagues, spread news or tell classic yarns.

It's these stories, the urban legends of the comics community, that this little book is about: the tales that are told late at night in the convention pro bar, the anecdotes, outrageous, funny or downright weird, that deserve to be documented for posterity.

These stories aren't usually reported in comic fanzines, nor are they the fodder of the online comic gossip columns, which seem to be mainly concerned with industry business rumours. They are modern myths and should be read as such. They evolve in the telling: events are exaggerated, details conveniently morph to plaster over half-remembered plot points and sometimes even the protagonists or locations are substituted for ones that just sound right at the time, sacrificing historical veracity for rhetorical effect. Some are demonstrably based on real situations and must be very close to the truth, whilst others are gross caricatures or distinctly apocryphal. It's up to you whether or not to believe that any of them are true, but it is true that they are told, and told again; the common currency of pro bar badinage, the raw material of the comic industry raconteur.

A couple of the stories have been covered by the fan press, such as the widely reported "feud" between Dave Sim and Jeff Smith but here I condense it and have an epilogue that isn't as well publicized, if at all.

A disproportionate number of these narratives are, of necessity, anecdotes about myself but I think that's perfectly legitimate: these are the stories that I tell in the pro bar and I know that some are repeated as I'm often asked to recount them by people who've heard second-hand versions.

I've avoided salacious tales of extra-marital affairs, strange sexual practices, such as the writer who has prostitutes dress up as his superheroines, and private sexual shenanigans, like the time a comics publisher had sex with a famous superhero artist on her desk while the intercom was still switched on and broadcasting to the main office. I'm mostly not concerned here with private lives. Mostly.

Neither have I included accounts of activities verging on the seriously criminal; such as publishers blatantly ripping off creators or the time a Vertigo artist spiked a rival artist's drink with acid. He never worked for the company again, by the way. If you want an account of how Bob Wood, ironically enough the artist of *Crime Does Not Pay*, murdered a woman in the late fifties and was subsequently murdered by some ex-cons, or how Greg Brooks, artist of *The Crimson Avenger*, battered his common-law wife to death in the eighties, do a websearch.

With one or two minor exceptions, you won't find the stories in this book on the internet. One of these exceptions is the scandalous Granada Comic Festival incident which, although reported in detail by Eric Reynolds on the *Comic Journal* website, demanded inclusion here nevertheless. You'll see why when you read it.

Although they are embellished for print, I've striven to keep the pro bar anecdotal style, switching tenses and often being intentionally vulgar. Readers who only know my work from *The Tale of One Bad Rat* or perhaps my new graphic novel *Alice in Sunderland* may be shocked at some of the language and subject matter of some of these legends but, apart from recommending that this tome be eschewed by persons of fragile sensibilities and that it certainly should be kept as far as possible from the eyes of babes and maiden aunts, there's bugger all that I can do about it. I'm afraid that I worked in underground comics for my first five years in this business and am, perforce, as common as muck.

To any creators who, to their horror, discover that they are the subject of one or more of these tales, take heart from Oscar Wilde's famous epigram: "There is only one thing in life worse than being talked about, and that is not being talked about." To those who feel disappointed because they've been left out, tell me your stories next time we meet. If the book, by some freakish fluke of the free market, becomes an   international best-seller, I'll write another and include them in that. After all, we're both in the same racket.

-Bryan Talbot
Sunderland, November 2006

CHAPTER ONE

BEER! SAUNA! NAKED MEN!

There are proportionately very few creators around who've made a fortune creating comics. The vast majority of pros just make a regular living, one that might vanish at any time if a publisher who owes you money goes bust or, for some reason, the comic company you've worked for solidly for a few years suddenly decides that you're passé and stops giving you work. This has happened to more of my colleagues than I care to contemplate.

However, there is one big perk that comes with the job: several times a year (with any luck) you'll be invited to a foreign convention or comics festival as a guest or by a publisher to promote your books. Admittedly you have to actually enjoy these things to think of them as a perquisite. I do and regard them as free holidays and very often the organisers do make sure there is some tourism or time to chill out built into your schedule.

Conventions are usually commercial events organised by small groups of fans or industry professionals that usually take place in one venue, often a hotel, and tend to last for just two or three days. As well as comic retailers' rooms, there'll be at least a few talks, panel discussions and perhaps a movie programme.

Festivals tend to be non-profit-making and hosted by the arts council or municipality of a town or city and take place in several venues dotted around the center, the idea being to bring in tourists who help the local economy by spending their cash there. They last from three days to, in the case of *Amadora* in Portugal, three weeks. As well as comic dealers and publishers, they'll also have at least one exhibition of comic art plus talks, discussions, films and often an award ceremony.

The biggest convention is the San Diego *Comicon*, held in that city's convention center–a huge airplane hangar of a joint about an eighth of a mile long–and the con fills it. With an attendance of over two hundred thousand fans and pros every year, and rising, it's become somewhat a victim of its own success with big movie and computer game companies starting to dominate the center by taking massive booths to promote their products. True, comic publishers such as DC, Dark Horse, Image and Marvel also have large and impressive booths, complete with banks of TV screens, life-size models of superheroes and other props but, rightly or wrongly, there's definitely a perception of the event being hijacked.

Still, it's held in a nice city with nice palm trees and a nice harbour and the weather's baking hot. At night you can watch cockroaches scuttling around on the sidewalk outside the posh restaurants on the waterfront. And it's a great event at which to meet people, including famous comic creators.

The first couple of times I attended in the eighties, I met a personal hero, the artist Jack Kirby, the prolific co-creator of Captain America, the Fantastic Four, X-men, and hundreds of other characters. He was such a lovely old guy I wanted to give him a hug. In fact I did. A young kid came up, seven or eight years old, and asked him for an autograph, which he happily supplied–in marked contrast to Bob Kane, creator of Batman, who arrived five minutes later and had a brief word with Jack before passing on. He was surrounded by four black-suited minders wearing shades who pushed fans away if they tried to approach him.

"Stay away from Mister Kane!" they snarled. "No autographs!"

San Diego was the first time I met classic artists such as Gene Colan, Gil Kane and Will Eisner. I got to know Will much better over several years after being guests together at the same festivals, from France to Brazil. To my utter amazement, he spontaneously wrote me an exceedingly complimentary letter after he read *The Tale of One Bad Rat* on the subject of its storytelling techniques. At one of the London UK Comic Art Conventions, I asked him if he could give me a quote that I could use on the back cover of *The Adventures of Luther Arkwright*.

"Write whatever the hell you like," he said, "and I'll swear I've said it!"

———————

I was once brought over to San Diego by the short-lived and laughably badly managed company Big Entertainment, for whom I was drawing *Teknophage*, created by Neil Gaiman and written by Rick Veitch. Another of their titles was *Mike Danger*, based on an original 1950s story by the internationally famous crime writer Mickey Spillane, whom I was astounded to actually meet there. He was just like I imagined him to be–a tough, wiry, white haired old guy with the manner of an ex-prizefighter who talked like a Brooklyn cabbie. That week, he was on a panel with *The Dark Knight Returns* and *Sin City* writer and artist Frank Miller and the loquacious and eloquent SF writer Harlan Ellison. Every time Harlan was holding forth, Mickey kept nudging Frank violently in the ribs and muttering to him "Big woids! Why does he keep usin' big woids?"

———

Cartoonist Harvey Kurtzman, the founding editor of *Mad*, probably now best known for his long-running *Playboy* sex comedy strip *Little Annie Fanny*, was actually a very shy man. One hot San Diego night in 1977 Lynn Chevely and Joyce Farmer, the publishers of a feminist erotic comic, the whimsically-titled *Tits and Clits*, and *Lost Girls* artist Melinda Gebbie jumped into the swimming pool at the El Cortez Hotel fully clothed. They were horsing around when they spotted Harvey walking by through the crowds of attendees surrounding the pool. Grabbing him by the legs, they unceremoniously pulled him into it. At this point a fanboy heard the splash and looked down from his hotel room balcony.

"Hey! It's Harvey Kurtzman!" he shouted, loud enough for all to hear. "He's in the pool with three chicks! And they all have their clothes on!"

Harvey was mortified as everybody crowded over to gape at him.

Other versions of this story have them naked but I heard this from eyewitnesses Trina Robbins, now a comics historian, and *Fables* inker Steve Leialoha.

———

At a UK Comic Art Convention in the eighties, as I had done with Will Eisner, I asked Harvey for a quote for the Luther Arkwright book. The third volume was yet to be published and I was collecting quotes for the back cover blurb. He perused the first two volumes, then wrote on a piece of paper "Bryan Talbot…super!" Succinct, but to the point, I thought and went away quite happy and the quote subsequently appeared on the cover. It was only after this I saw that every single Kurtzman quote promoting other artists at that time consisted of "(insert name of artist here)…super!"

———

Many comic artists have a skeleton in the closet–literally. I have one twelve inches high and a life-sized human skull, both made from plastic kits. I also have a life size skeleton made out of a cardboard kit, sold as an aid to medical students. As figurative artists we have to have at least a nodding acquaintance with human anatomy, something that no longer seems to concern so-called fine artists. I've even heard comic art described as the last bastion of figure drawing…but I'm wandering seriously off topic here.

So, anyway, **Watchmen** and **The Originals** artist Dave Gibbons, in San Diego for the Comicon is given a half life-size, anatomically perfect and realistically articulated plastic skeleton–a present from Frank Miller, bought at a medical store. Aimed at hard-up medical students who couldn't afford the life-sized model, it was marketed under the brand name "Mister Thrifty".

On the last day of the con, Dave's sitting on the steps outside and wondering how he can manage to carry the three foot box containing this wonderful drawing aid and his other luggage which, going from personal experience is, by this time, weighed down with dozens of books and comics acquired at the con. Paul Chadwick, writer and artist of **Concrete**, magically produces a spare pair of disposable carrying handles he happens to have in his briefcase. Gibbo loops the string attached to the handles around the box and voila, his problem is solved. Which is all fine and dandy until he's passing through LAX airport security a few hours later and he places the box containing Mister Thrifty onto the carry-on luggage conveyor belt.

The overweight lady watching the x-ray monitor, bored out of her skull, suddenly does an eye-popping double-take and screams, leaping out of her chair and sending it flying.

"JESUS-FUCKING-CHRIST-WHAT-THE-HELL!" she shrieks, clutching her heaving bosom. "How…how old was it?!"

Dave explains that it's not really a dead child and saunters off as the relieved security guards put their guns back in their holsters.

Denys Cowan, artist on **The Question** and one of the founders of Milestone Comics, a DC imprint designed to redress the balance in regard to the under-representation of African-Americans in comics, is an exceptionally cool bloke. At one San Diego, he'd made quite a bit of money selling comic artwork and drawing sketches and thought it would be a good idea to get some of it off his hands by settling his hotel bill in cash. Returning to his room, he was packing to leave when he heard a strange noise outside his door. He immediately whipped it open to find a Highway Patrolman pointing a gun straight at his face. It transpired that the hotel figured that a black man with cash equalled a drug dealer and had reported him. It took Denys a good twenty minutes to convince the cop that he'd earned the money honestly.

In the eighties, Canadian cartoonist Colin Upton attended a well-known publisher's party one night during the con. The company's public relations man repeatedly approached him, bottles of beer clutched in his hands, urging him to help himself.

"Hey, go for it!" the PR guy urged. "It's all free!"

Colin repeatedly declined the offer, as he doesn't drink. Eventually getting the message, the guy asked him where he was from. On discovering that Colin lived in Vancouver, without hesitation he asked him to buy some China White heroin when he got home and post it to him. China White had been in the news at the time because of the astonishing rate of fatal overdoses it had meted out to the junkie community of Vancouver's skid row. Apparently it was exceptionally pure and therefore devastatingly strong. Shocked, Colin informed him that it was responsible for several deaths but, to this dork, that only meant it was "good stuff".

"Those assholes are amateurs!" he sneered.

When Colin informed him that he wasn't about to become a drug dealer, the guy just couldn't understand his reluctance.

"Look," Colin continued, "I don't even know how or where to buy any drugs, never mind heroin!"

He stared at Colin in utter amazement.

"I don't believe it!" he said with unconcealed disgust. "You're an artist, right?"

Colin later produced a cartoon based on the incident for a Vancouver newspaper.

———

Colin was recently invited to a con in Victoria, British Columbia. The organisers had spared no expense flying in guests, covering their hotel bills and even giving them spending money and punters were accordingly charged twenty dollars a day entrance fee and extra for some programme items. The problem was, as far as Colin could discern, the con hadn't spent a single penny on advertising. The exhibitors easily outnumbered the fans. Colin was required to be at his table for twelve hours a day and he dutifully sat there, bored rigid, lucky if he sold one comic every few hours. Flipping through the events programme, he was astonished to discover that he was scheduled to give a talk on porno comics. Luckily, no one was attending the talks, so he just skipped it. The wrap party on the Sunday night had a distinctly surreal air as the organizers tried to pretend that the con hadn't been the most complete and utter disaster since The Titanic's last dance party.

———

Writer and artist of the graphic novel *Faith, a Fable* Bill Knapp also had an exceptionally crap con experience in the late nineties when he'd booked a table at the annual Mid-Ohio con to sell his self-published comic *The Furies*.

Arriving early to see where he'd been allocated a space, he found that he'd been placed in a corner, next to Uncle Scrooge artist Don Rosa and with Kurt Busiek and Brent Anderson at right angles to him–there to sign their best-selling *Astro City*.

"Great!" thought Bill, "I'm in with the comic stars! There's bound to be a hell of a lot of traffic through here!"

Picturing himself picking up lots of passing trade, Bill cheerfully set up his table and prepared to deal with the rush of fans when the big names arrived. A little like *Astro City*, his comic series had a realistic take on superheroes so their fans might possibly like it.

The room was pretty quiet till Kurt and Brent arrived late morning and sat down to sign. Immediately the room was inundated with hundreds of superhero fans, surging to their corner and forming a huge line that stretched from there to the entrance–a line that had its apex practically right in front of Bill's table, immediately cutting him off from any of the other punters wandering around the room.

To begin with, Bill tried to engage the fans in the line in conversation, trying to show them his comics. He tried any and all means of attracting their attention short of jumping naked onto the table and juggling burning groundhogs while whistling The Star-Spangled Banner. They just weren't interested. They were queuing to see their heroes and were totally focused on their imminent audience with these godlike beings. The few superhero fans that did give *The Furies* a cursory glace could immediately glean that it wasn't their cup of tea. For one thing, it wasn't published by Marvel, Image or DC. For another it was in black and white and, anyway, the female characters didn't have tits the size of Nebraska.

When Don Rosa turned up in the afternoon it got even worse, the Disney fans forming another line at right-angles to the first, effectively trapping Bill in the corner and sealing him off from the rest of the known universe. It was a long day.

That night Bill asked the organisers whether he could move to another table but it was impossible–they were all booked. On the Sunday morning it was clear that the same thing was going to happen again and by noon Bill gave it up as a bad job and went home.

―――――――

At a con in Dallas, *Batman and The Bogie Man* writer Alan Grant spent an evening with Batman artist Kelley Jones and comic artist and cover painter Bo Hampton (though in some versions, it's his brother Scott). After dinner, they carried on drinking expensive Chablis long into the night until an argument broke out between Alan and Bo about the artistic merits of comic art. Sozzled, Alan was being deliberately provocative, insisting that all comic artists, both good and bad, were hacks. Taking great exception to this, Bo picked up his wine and poured it over Alan's head. A scuffle ensued until Kelley Jones separated the pair.

The following morning, each sheepishly apologised to the other.

"You see, I'm a redneck," said Bo. "I'm not used to drinking wine, only beer."

"Well, I'm Scottish," said Alan. "We're not used to drinking at all."

From 1985 to 1998 the premier British convention was the UK Comic Art Convention or, as it was known, UKCAC, run by Frank Plowright and Hassan Yusuf. During its heyday it was the best con ever. For pros, it was be there or be square and at night the London hotel bar was usually filled with as many as two hundred comic professionals including most of the Brit pack and many big name artists from America and Europe. It was so successful that for several years in the nineties, Frank and Hass ran a second convention in Glasgow, GLASCAC.

It was at one UKCAC that Alan Moore was so doggedly mobbed by fans that he refused to go to any comic convention again. In an incident infamous in the comic industry, the fans were so insistent that they followed him into the bathroom and lined up outside his toilet cubicle, shoving comics under the door for him to sign.

This is the point when he raised his eyes heavenwards and mentally screamed "What the FUCK am I doing here?"

Later, in the con's green room, he was waiting to appear on a *Watchmen* panel with Dave Gibbons and talking with *Sandman* writer and now famous novelist Neil Gaiman to arrange an interview. At that time, Neil hadn't begun his comic career and was still a journalist. Neil admitted to Alan that he'd like to become a comic writer and Alan looked back at him in horror.

"Look," he said, "out there is a dealers' room. It's full of comics. I'd love to go and buy some. But I can't. There's a thousand people out there and they all want to talk to me."

At the same con, Neil spotted Frank Miller emerging from the bathroom, visibly shocked. He'd been relieving himself at the urinal when a teenage fan held a copy of Dark Knight between him and the porcelain and asked him to sign it.

"What did he want me to do? Sign it with my dick?" said Frank incredulously.

A danger for foreign guests was the London traffic, a major road being in-between the convention site and the pro hotel. In Britain we drive on the left side of the road. Most other countries drive on the wrong side of the road. When Roy Thomas, writer of **Conan the Barbarian** and **X-Men** and one time editor-in-chief of Marvel Comics, was crossing to the hotel, returning from an early morning jog, he looked left to check for oncoming traffic. The road was clear so he stepped out–directly in front of a motorcycle coming from the right. His leg was broken and he spent the remainder of his time in the UK in hospital.

One event at UKCAC still remains vivid in the memory of dozens of now ageing and most probably senile fans. This was the occasion when a glamorous American publisher was on a panel discussion, resplendent in full power-dress, with wide padded shoulders, high heels and immaculately coiffured hair. She was also wearing black lace panties and black nylon stockings with a garter belt, as all the fans in the audience could clearly see as she unselfconsciously sprawled her legs in a most unladylike manner. She just didn't realise that the sheet covering the on-stage table she was sitting at didn't hang down on the side between her legs and them. There was a minor commotion as pop-eyed fanboys fought each other off to get to the front of the crowd. Apparently photos of the spectacular view were circulated next day. I was on the balcony at the time so can't really claim to be an eyewitness.

The UKCAC hotel bar closed late, somewhere approaching breakfast time. In fact it was not unknown for some con attendees to spend the night in the bar, rather than pay for a room. Some fans, of course, would book a room and reduce the cost by splitting it with a dozen others, bodies covering every inch of the floor and the room reverberating with snores and farts.

At the bar one evening, Dave Gibbons, Alan Grant and DC editor Mike Carlin were chatting when Alan mentioned that his preferred method of relaxation was the sensory-deprivation floatation tank, positioned just where the altar used to be in the twelfth century church he was then living in. For some reason, Dave found this highly amusing and started ragging him about it. Alan responded by being equally disparaging about Dave's long standing practice of the oriental discipline of Tai Chi. The argument became heated as the insult stakes cranked up until it seemed as if the thing would come to blows. Mike Carlin knew exactly how to calm things down. He went to the bar and returned bearing fresh pints of beer, thus quelling the rages of these two experts in the art of relaxation.

Judge Dredd and *Doctor Who* novelist Dave Stone was, for some reason perhaps connected with what some people perceived as his insufferable manner, almost universally disliked–hence the pro bar motto "David Stone sits alone". Perversely, he seemed to invite and enjoy the irritation he stimulated by being deliberately exasperating.

One night, under the influence of an inordinate amount of alcohol, he passed out in a chair in the bar. His handkerchief was hanging out of his pocket and was noticed by *Preacher* artist Steve Dillon who whipped out his zippo and set it on fire. As his hankie went up in flames Dave slept on until Steve picked up somebody's pint of bitter and doused him with it, putting out the conflagration. I say "somebody's" because I just can't imagine Steve wasting his own in such an irresponsible manner.

A different version has Steve putting the fire out with his hands and burning them in the process, though I prefer the above.

On another occasion Dave passed out again after getting completely rat-arsed and, while he was dead to the world, *Preacher* writer Garth Ennis used an indelible marker to write, backwards, an extremely rude word relating to female genitalia across his forehead–an explicit message to him every time he looked in a mirror for the next few days. John McCrea then used the pen to decorate the rest of his face with obscene doodles.

When John had finished, Garth took a close-up photo of the comatose Stone and next morning had a few dozen copies made and sold them to fans at the con.

After a very long stint in the con bar, John, artist of *Troubled Souls* and *Hitman*, decided to call it a night. He returned to his room a little concerned, as Marvel editor Joe Quesada, whom he'd arranged to meet there, hadn't shown up. Stripping off to go to bed, he suddenly heard Joe passing by, chatting to someone in the corridor outside. Anxious to have a word, he dashed to the door and cracked it open but they'd passed on around a corner. He took a few steps out to peer around it and was about to call out when he saw that it wasn't Joe after all. He turned back, only to find that the door had closed behind him, leaving him stark bollock naked and locked out of his room. Tiptoeing along the corridors in the middle of the night, he managed to make it all the way to the lobby without being spotted and made for the cover of a potted palm. The reception desk was only accessible across a wide expanse of open foyer, stranding John behind the plant for quarter of an hour until a doorman walked by and John could whistle him over to request a key and something to cover his assets.

In 1990, a group of creators from Britain and Finland were taken to Murmansk in the then Soviet Union on a sort of comics cultural exchange visit. This involved an interminable and epic journey over freezing seas and snowbound

roads that I'm not even going to begin to recount. The hotel in Murmansk was grim, to say the least, and the food even grimmer, leaving the invitees nothing to do but drink vodka and cheap Russian champagne. I met the British contingent of the party as they arrived back in London, still laden with their baggage, for the last day of a UKCAC. They resembled a group of shell-shocked refugees from the Russian Front.

After one Murmansk evening of record-breaking vodka consumption, top British cartoonist Hunt Emerson retired to his bed exhausted as the party raged on. In the middle of the night he was suddenly awoken by an insistent hammering on his bedroom door.

"Hunt! HUNT! Quick! It's an emergency!"

He recognised the voice of Kristina, the very attractive Finnish PR person.

"Oh my God!" he thought, reeling from his bed, still drunk and half-asleep. "The KGB have come for us! The gulag awaits!"

Stark naked, he flung open the door to be confronted with Kristina and a large group of her colleagues.

"W-What is it?" he asked.

"I need a bag for my shopping," she said. "Do you have a spare one?"

Dazed, Hunt staggered back inside, dug out a plastic bag and, still naked, handed it to her.

"No," she said. "It's too small. Thank you."

———————

One GLASCAC, on the morning of a night before, Dave Gibbons and a few other *2000AD* stalwarts are nursing their hangovers in the hotel breakfast room when the art editor of the comic, Robin Smith, breezes up to the table and joins them. He's remarkably perky for this ungodly hour and saunters over to the breakfast bar to get some nosh. I've always been astonished at the way con hotels can magically turn bacon into something resembling shoe leather, transmute sausages into reinforced rubber and cook eggs in such a precise fashion as to render the egg whites runny while baking the yolks rock-hard. Anyhow, Robin returns with a plate that's positively heaving with   anything that he's managed to pile onto it: eggs, bacon, sausages, black puddings, fried bread, hash browns, tomatoes, mushrooms, beans, ketchup, mustard, you name it. He plonks it down on the table, making light of the meagre rations the assembled afflicted are prodding at disinterestedly with their forks.

On sitting down, he performs what seems like a consummate juggling trick that's guaranteed to cheer them up: his elbow catches the plate in such a way that it does a perfect hundred and eighty degree flip and lands directly on his lap with a disgusting squelch. This caused so much hilarity that it did indeed lighten the sombre mood of the whole group. He was wearing the only pair of trousers he'd brought so, for the next couple of hours, was imprisoned in his room while he scrubbed his jeans and blasted them with the hair drier.

———————

Sometimes comic creators are invited to "memorabilia" conventions. These are usually huge events dedicated to "media" and feature stars from cult movies and TV shows. You'll get original *Star Trek* veterans and Hammer Horror scream queens signing alongside the out-of-focus fourth guy along the Death Star control console from *Return of the Jedi* selling autographed photos of himself for twenty dollars a hit. I've met the likes of Lou Ferrigno–TV's Incredible Hulk–and James Marsters–Spike from

Buffy the Vampire Slayer-at these sort of events. James' female fans screamed the place down every time he hit the stage in a re-enactment of Beatlemania at its height.

At a memorabilia con in London a couple of years ago, *Albion* co-writer John Reppion was paying the price for eating a very dodgy curry the night before. His guts in horrific turmoil, he sought out the only available toilet in the guest reception lounge and parked himself there for a good half hour until his bowels were empty and his rectal rebellion was quelled, despite an intermittent but polite knocking on the door of the cubicle. On opening the door, he was confronted by the glamorous Charisma Carpenter–Cordelia from Buffy–who was apparently also in dire need of urgent relief.

So glad was she that John had vacated the hot seat, she hugged him, a total stranger, there and then before rushing into the confined area before John had a chance to say "I'd leave it a couple of minutes if I were you!"

Though it was the biggest UK con, with an attendance of two or three thousand, the UKCACs were much smaller than their American counterparts but correspondingly more intimate. Since UKCAC, the biggest British con is now the Bristol Comic Expo each May. Others include the annual small press convention, Caption, held in Oxford in August. Again, its American counterpart, Washington's SPX con in October is much larger but even most US cons are small events when compared with the biggest European Comics Festival, held in Angoulême near Bordeaux, which attracts over a quarter of a million visitors every January.

Now in its thirty-third year, Angoulême really is a phenomenon, with the whole town taking part. Apart from the large marquees filled with international publishers' booths, distributors and retailers, there seems to be exhibitions everywhere - from the post office, town hall and cathedral all the way down to bars and cafes and comic displays in shop windows.

Because of the festival, Angoulême is also home to the imposing Centre National de la Bande Dessinée et de l'Image–the purpose-built French national center for comic art, with its large exhibition spaces, library, comic album store and workshops. The Angoulême theatre in the center of town hosts the prestigious festival award ceremony. Signings by comic artists are announced over loudspeakers in the streets, many of which feature permanent murals designed by top European comic artists. Even the street signs are in the shape of speech balloons. If you're seriously into comics, this is the place to go.

Every year the French media covers the event extensively, with TV crews filming documentaries and interviewing fans and creators and the national newspaper *Liberation* featuring a special pull-out Angoulême supplement. Yes, it's a big cultural event. In France the comic medium is referred to as L'Art Neuvième–"The Ninth Art"–and some French comic artists are awarded their Medal of Honour for services to art. This is quite different from how comics are perceived in the UK, where they are still thought of, on the whole, as having only marginally more artistic value than patterned toilet roll paper.

Each year a country is chosen as a theme for the festival, which hosts many of that nation's comic creators and stages a major exhibition of their work. The first time I attended was nearly twenty years ago when it was British Year. The exhibition was titled "God Save the Comics!" and dozens of UK writers and artists were invited and flown over for the event.

I don't know whether the jet taking us over had been specially chartered or not but it was completely filled with Brit comic talent. I remember thinking at the time that, if the thing crashed, it would have been the end of the British comic industry. With writers such as Alan Moore, Jamie Delano, Pete Milligan, Alan Grant, John Wagner and Grant Morrison on board, along with artists the likes of Brian Bolland, Dave Gibbons, Steve Dillon, Glenn Fabry and David Lloyd and the editors and publishers of many comics including the British SF weekly *2000AD* and the monthly magazines *Deadline* and *Escape*, the landscape of comics today would be very different if they'd all suddenly perished. As the plane was taxiing towards the runway, it suddenly and startlingly slammed to a halt. After a few minutes it carried on and the captain's voice came over the speakers to apologize. His explanation was that he'd braked because a field mouse was running across the runway in front of the plane. I don't think that anyone believed him somehow.

During the festival, Grant Morrison was being interviewed on stage. The French translator had so much trouble with Grant's Glaswegian accent that he required a second translator to put Grant's words into a version of English he understood.

———————

Oddly enough, many of us were guests again a couple of years later, when it was American Year, as most of us were then working for American publishers. Since, I like to attend Angoulême every two or three years. I space out the visits because I'm very fond of the ancient town and the event and don't want going there ever to turn into a chore. It can be very hard work, especially when you're doing sketches at publishers' booths for hours at a time. Everybody there seems to want a free drawing, whether they've heard of you or not.

One Angoulême, Hunt Emerson is doing les petites dédicasses for a line of punters. A teenage girl is next in line and asks Hunt for a drawing.

"Do you have a sketch book?" he asks.

She lifts up her tee-shirt and points to her right breast.

"Draw on here."

Hunt conscientiously responds by drawing his Firkin the Cat character on her bare boob with his indelible marker, employing her nipple as Firkin's nose.

A big difference between European and Stateside comic events is that, on this side of the pond, the punters expect, and get, sketches from their favorite artists for nothing–even from really big names such as Moebius, who'll sit drawing for them for hours. In the US most artists charge, though a distinction is made between a pencilled and inked illustration and a quick scribble, which is, generally speaking, free.

Jim Steranko who, in the sixties, was the hugely influential artist of **Nick Fury, Agent of SHIELD** and, more recently **Chandler: Red Tide** abruptly stopped doing sketches for free back in the early seventies. His epiphany happened at one con when he was besieged by fans so numerous it was obvious that only a small percentage would actually come away with a picture. He completed inking a sketch of Captain America and handed it over to the grinning fan at the head of the line who promptly turned around and held it up.

"Steranko sketch, fifty dollars!" he shouted and quickly sold it before Jim's astonished eyes.

The free sketches that many of us do for fans frequently end up on eBay, one reason why I always dedicate them to the person requesting the drawing. I've several framed sketches myself, by greats including Moebius, Hugo Pratt and Will Eisner, but, of course, would never part with them. Offers considered.

As I said, Angoulême is the big one but there are other French festivals, such as Grenoble, Blois and Lille, and many others around Europe, the largest being Germany's Erlangen Festival and the one at Barcelona in Spain.

One of my favorites is the Lucca festival in Tuscany, the first foreign convention that I was invited to over twenty years ago and one I've attended a few times since, once having an exhibition of my Bad Rat artwork there. Lucca's a beautiful walled medieval town but, these days, the festival has grown too large for the center and is held in the sports arena outside the city walls.

I met **Brat Pack** and **Rare Bit Fiends** writer and artist Rick Veitch at Lucca on my first visit. He'd recently done his first graphic novel, the comic adaptation of Speilberg's movie **1941** with Steve Bissette, while still a student at the Joe Kubert Comic Art School in New York.

This was the first time Rick had been outside the States and Joe, without mentioning it to him, phones his old compadre Hugo Pratt. Hugo, primarily known for his Corto Maltese stories, was a comic artist and writer of not only great stature in international comics but also in physical terms.

Joe says to him "Hugo, one of my boys is going over to Italy. Can you take care of him while he's in Lucca?"

"Sure," says the man.

Anyhow, the week goes by and Pratt doesn't say a word to Rick, never even approaches him. On the Saturday night, a bunch of us are in the lobby of the Hotel Napoleon, having drunk dry the free booze at the tequila sunrise party laid on by the festival. Dave Gibbons had disappeared to his room and returned with the bottle of duty-free brandy he picked up on the way over and is passing it around. *Groo* artist Sergio Aragones is drawing, in fact we all are, in each other's sketchbooks.

At this point, the imposing form of Hugo Pratt looms into the lobby. He walks straight over to Rick and clamps his big hand on Rick's shoulder. Rick turns around, startled.

"Veitch?" enquires Pratt.

Rick confirms, Hugo jerks his head in the direction of the front door and marches off outside.

Rick's wife, Sindy, says "What does he want?"

"No idea," says Rick and follows him out.

Outside, no Pratt. He looks around and sees Hugo stomping off down the street. Running to catch up with him, he asks what's going on. Pratt just puts a finger to his lips and beckons Rick to follow.

They walk a couple of blocks and Pratt heads down an alleyway with Rick in tow. At the end is a house with steps on the outside, running up to a door on the first floor. Reaching the top of the stairs, Hugo brings his heavy fist down on the door a few times until a couple of bolts are pulled back and the door opens a crack. A couple of phrases of whispered Italian later and they're inside. As Rick's eyes slowly get accustomed to the gloom, Hugo has a brief and incomprehensible exchange with a big Italian momma, turns on his heel and exits.

Only now does Rick discern that he's in the company of a bevy of heavily made-up Italian ladies sitting around in their underwear. It's a brothel! This is Hugo's idea of "taking care of him"!

Rick hastily makes his excuses and returns to the hotel.

It was during this week that Hugo drew me the sketch I mentioned earlier. I met him only once again, several years later at the Barcelona festival, shortly before he died, and he was looking decidedly ill. When Hugo died, I had a call from the *Comics Journal*. They were looking for reminiscences of him to include in their next issue. I immediately told them that they really should contact Rick Veitch as he had a great Hugo Pratt story. Some months later, I was with Rick at a con in Dallas and asked him if they'd been in touch with him about it. Unfortunately, they hadn't, so there it is for the first time.

From Hell artist Eddie Campbell tells of a time at a Swiss Comics Festival when he received a message from Hugo asking if they could meet the following morning at the comic art exhibition. Eddie was puzzled, never having met him before and wondered what the great man could possibly want.

Next morning, he's up and breakfasted in plenty of time and is about to set off when he bumps into British comics historian the late Denis Gifford in the lobby.

"Can't stop to chat," he tells Denis. "I've a meeting with Hugo Pratt".

Giffo maintains he's an old friend of Pratt's and hasn't seen him for years and asks if he can tag along. Eddie agrees and they leave the hotel, meeting outside Giffo's successor as Britain's incumbent comics expert, Paul Gravett, who's very excited at the prospect of meeting Hugo Pratt and asks if he can come too.

"Why not?" says Eddie and off they go, coming across a group of fellow festival attendees in the street.

"We're going to see Hugo Pratt," boasts Giffo, drawing them along in his wake and, as they walk through the town to the exhibition, Eddie realizes that more and more people are glomming onto the group, making a veritable procession with himself in the lead. By the time they reach the gallery, they are a vast chattering multitude, all wanting to meet Hugo. They flood in, filling the place. Either he's in here, obscured by the crowd, or he's seen them coming and buggered off. Whichever way, Eddie doesn't get to meet him.

Towards the end of the festival, Eddie pops into the exhibition for a last quick look around and there's Hugo, deep in conversation with someone, walking round the gallery. They stop in front of Eddie's page and he sneaks over to eavesdrop on what they are saying about it, hoping to solve the mystery of Pratt's interest in him.

He's rewarded by overhearing Hugo say "Why does he put all these bloody little bits of Letratone (Zippertone in the States) all over his pictures?"

Eddie told me this story in San Diego but has since told it in strip form in his graphic novel *How to be an Artist*.

At one time the Lucca Festival was organised by Rinaldo Trahini, a controversial figure in Italian comics who once reprinted Marvel Comics for several years without, it is said, ever paying a penny in royalties. He also had a reputation for bringing artists over from the States, getting them to promote his comics with signings and TV interviews, then never reimbursing them for their time or travel expenses. Several years ago, amid accusations of corruption, he split with Lucca after a confrontation with Hugo Pratt and now runs the large convention in Rome, though it has to be said that it's a pretty soulless affair. It's basically a glorified comic and computer game mart that takes place in a miserable modern industrial estate outside the city, far from Rome's incredible buildings and antiquities.

The Gijón Festival in Asturias, the "Green Coast" of the North of Spain, is a festival that is quite unique. It's actually the longest running European comics festival, begun in 1969 and still organised under the guiding hand of Faustino Rodriguez Arbesú. I say "unique" because it's purely a cultural event. This means that there are no publishers booths or retailers' stalls. In fact, with the exception of the annual comic art exhibition, nothing happens during the day at all (apart from trips to tourist spots and large lunches for the guests). Everything in the week-long festival takes place after six-thirty at night in the theatre in the town center where, on average, three guests per night are interviewed by the audience, with the assistance of a roving microphone and a translator.

On the Saturday night is the flamboyant award ceremony when the Haxturs are presented. Haxtur was a famous Spanish barbarian comic hero in the sixties and the awards named after him are statuettes of the character in bronze on a marble base. They're one of the most handsome comic awards, looking a little like Oscars and weighing approximately three tons each. In 1996, in lieu of an acceptance speech, portly Hulk and Spiderman writer Peter David delighted the audience by spontaneously dancing the Macarena.

Getxo, in Bilbao, down the coast in the Basque region, is also a great venue and the people are lovely but it's more of a convention than a festival. Still, you do get to visit the Guggenheim Museum there, an incredible building.

A few years ago I was a guest, along with *Cages* artist and writer Dave McKean, at the small but very pleasant festival in Palma where, apart from giving my *Bad Rat* presentation, the time was spent being wined and dined around the island of Mallorca and being taken to see some breath-taking views.

When my wife Mary and I arrived at the airport, we met the festival people and waited a while for the plane bringing another guest, Spanish cartoonist Das Pastoras. His style and humour is a little like Glen Larson's but much better drawn. In the minibus that collected us he produced his numerous sketchbooks, all filled with the gorgeous full colour illustrations that he uses in his work. We were driven to the cultural center, where we met the staff, and were taken to a very nice restaurant across the road for lunch.

Two hours later, we returned to the minibus to find that some bastard had broken into it and stolen Mary's leather coat and Das Pastoras' suitcase containing the slide show he was intending to give at the festival and all his sketchbooks chock full of original art. The coat was no big thing and we got it replaced on the travel insurance a few weeks later in Milan but the sketchbooks were irreplaceable.

The organisers were up at the crack of dawn next day, scouring the local flea markets in the hope of finding the books but to no avail. If they had been mine I would have been devastated and so, presumably, was Das Pastoras but every time we saw him during the remainder of the festival, he acted as if nothing had happened and was disconcertingly jolly.

There are many cons and small festivals in Belgium, Germany and Scandinavia but my favorite is Kemi in Finland.

Kemi is the northernmost comics festival in the world, held every May, just south of the Artic Circle. It's a real fun con, the Finns notoriously capable of drinking everyone else beneath the table. I was a guest in the mid-nineties and met for the first time fellow guests Jeff Smith and Vijaya Iyer in the airport in Helsinki as we waited for the connecting flight north.

Coincidentally, on the flight I was seated next to the other guest, the frighteningly talented Anders Westerberg from Sweden.

"Are you Bryan Talbot?" he asked.

"How did you know?" I said.

"You look like an artist." he replied. I still don't know what he meant by this.

Usually, as a guest, you arrive at a festival and are immediately immersed in the event but on this occasion they brought us to Kemi two days early and drove us north for six hours, right up into Lapland to almost literally chill out before the thing started. The Laps have no word for "wilderness": it's just where they live. Once the minibus had to brake sharply to avoid hitting an unbelievably massive moose that was lumbering across the road.

There, the silence is total. After the end of the tree line, there are no birds, it's on no airline flight path and traffic is virtually non-existent. At night we stood on the veranda of the large wooden house just listening to the silence. On the second night we briefly heard a hoot owl. It must have been about ten miles away but we could hear its call carried on the air. In May it never really goes dark and, sitting on the A-frame swing outside at half past midnight, we watched the sun go down then curve upwards again till, by one o'clock, it was dawn.

The house is the home of a Finnish fine artist named Reijo Raekallio and doubles as an art gallery. In the skiing season, he and his wife do bed and breakfast and he sells his paintings to visitors. There's a small complex of large log cabins built by Reijo, one of which is his studio. At this time he'd just produced a comic book in time for Kemi.

This jaunt was one of the most pleasant experiences I've ever had at a con or festival. The con organisers, including artist Ilpo Koskela, and Anders were great company and Jeff and Vijaya are two of my favorite people. Jeff's epic fantasy graphic novel *Bone* is a marvel of comic story-telling and fluid linework. We ate delicious reindeer stew, drank wine and, one day, Reijo fired up his sauna.

This was a proper "smoke sauna" in which he burned wood for about eight hours before we went in. By that point the fire had died away but the large rocks that it had heated were mad-hot, hotter than any commercial sauna. The beer bottles got so hot that they burnt our lips when we took a swig. You can only take around ten minutes in there at a time and, in the antechamber where we cooled down between sessions, our skins pumped out steam like kettles on full boil, illuminated by the laser beam of sunshine that streamed through the small side window. It felt as though my very bones were hot. Afterwards we rolled naked in the snow. You have to–to close up your pores. Honest. This isn't as painful as it sounds, as you're that hot you're melting the bloody stuff as you roll in it.

The Finns really do have a thing about saunas. Even many small houses have one in their bathroom. Once in Tuurku I was taken to a pub in the sticks where my hosts, the owners of its Cosmic Comic Café, rented the in-house sauna for an hour. A crate of beer was supplied (you just pay for what you drink).

In the changing room I asked about the hourly rates that were framed on the wall. There were rates for parties of various numbers all the way down to two, which made it plain that if you met someone in the pub that you fancied, you could hire the sauna and immediately consummate the relationship. I'm not joking. Below the rate for two persons was a list of condom prices. Somehow I couldn't see this happening in a British pub.

One night we hit a posher sauna at a five star hotel in the city center and CCC regular Sami, an extremely affable and entertaining individual, looked out across the river from the changing room at the Civic Center of Tuurku where, visible through its large windows, a speech was being given by a politician to a large audience: part of his campaign during the local elections then taking place. The speaker had his back to the window, the audience facing the hotel. Sami immediately whipped off his towel, ran outside onto the balcony and mooned the lot of them. The politician spun around, wondering what they were all gaping at and Sami ran back to the doors, stark naked, only to find that they'd closed automatically, leaving him stranded in full view of the crowd. Someone was eventually good enough to open them again before he shattered the glass by hammering on it to get back in.

On the Saturday night at Kemi, the guests were taken to the annual festival party where, while the other attendees danced and drank, we were scheduled to have the traditional dinner with the Mayor and his wife in an impressive wood-panelled private room. Unfortunately the Mayor couldn't make it and the local sports councillor had been forcibly drafted in as a last minute substitute. He was a big burly dude with a drooping moustache and a seventies' bouffant hairdo who obviously had no interest in the festival and even less in comics. When we arrived, he and his wife, who were in their mid-fifties, were already half-plastered, swaying slightly and gulping wine as the organisers tried make polite conversation with them in the bar.

It was time for dinner. I found myself sitting at one end of the table, facing the councillor and next to his wife.

He banged his fist on the table and pronounced loudly in English "I have something to say!"

He then proceeded to give the official speech of welcome in Finnish, though his gruff and begrudging manner was distinctly at odds with the delivery of the smiling, soft-spoken translator, Tuula Tervaharju, sitting next to him.

Waiting for our food, he banged the table again. "I have something to say!"

He rambled on, slurred and with a sullen edge to his voice. Tuula suddenly winced, dropped her smile and gulped before attempting to begin. She was having obvious difficulty in paraphrasing into genteel English what turned out to be an ugly diatribe against people with AIDS and sick people in general, struggling to make it sound pleasant and conversational and leaving out the swear words.

And so it proceeded: every five minutes or so he would thump the table and make a misanthropic pronouncement which the poor Tuula had to render palatable through clenched teeth.

Meanwhile, to my right, his wife was bored witless, staring vacantly at the wall and taking a hefty slug of white wine at regular ten second intervals. She could speak fluent English but had said nothing since we'd entered the dining room. By the end of the main course I had the distinct impression that I wasn't being a very good guest. I should be a gentleman and give her some attention, rather than just chatting with the other guests and con people. I turned to her and she stared blankly back.

I was desperately trying to think of something to talk about. In a burst of Wildean eloquence I came up with "I have a rat in my hotel room."

Her eyes widened and her lip curled in disgust.

"Oh, it's you has the rat, is it?" she said.

It was at this point that I noticed the councillor, sitting opposite, was glowering, looking daggers at me from beneath heavy black brows.

I actually did have a rat in my room. The news must have spread. The next day Anders, Jeff and I were to be interviewed individually for a Finnish TV documentary on the festival and I thought it would be cool if I did my piece with a rat sitting on my shoulder. *The Tale of One Bad Rat* had just been published there and I thought it would be a nice visual touch. So I'd visited the pet shop in Kemi and hired a rat, its cage and food for the weekend. As it turned out, the rat was bloody useless. It was so shy it ran away every time I tried to pick it up. The camera crew had to be content with filming it through the bars. Anyhow...

The councillor's wife was now frowning, staring into space and knocking back wine at an even faster rate. Had I inadvertently upset her? How could I make it up? I asked to borrow Jeff's sketchpad, took out a page and did a drawing of a cute rat on it. I wanted to dedicate it so I asked her name.

"Pie-kee," she said. "Pie-kee."

She put her hands together as if in prayer and wriggled them from side to side. It took me a few seconds to realize that she was miming a fish. She took the pen and wrote her name on her nakpin: "Pike" (pronounced "Pie-kee"). Ah, right. So I wrote "For Pike" across the top of the page and passed her the picture.

Her response was startling. She held it up at arms' length and stared at it, wide-eyed and eyebrows raised, for a couple of seconds, then at me. She repeated this action many times, switching her gaze between the sketch and myself and saying nothing. Her husband was grinding his teeth. He looked as though he was ready to fling himself across the table and throttle me.

Jeff had been watching the exchange and was now concerned that I'd insulted her somehow. He grabbed the pad and quickly did a sketch of Bone - Bone in love, his eyes heavenward and with little hearts pulsing from his body—inscribed "To Pike" above it and placed it on the table before her.

Her shocked expression didn't change. If anything she looked more manic. She picked up Jeff's sketch and held it up alongside mine, switching her gaze from one to the other, then to me and Jeff in rapid succession as if she couldn't believe somebody would be so—what? Daring? Daft? Magnanimous? Sycophantic? I just couldn't read her expression—as to draw her a sketch.

There was a loud crash as the councillor's fist hit the table, rattling the crockery.

"I HAVE SOMETHING TO SAY!" he snarled.

Tuula informed us that he was very insistent that we ordered our dessert course right this very minute.

"I don't want one, thank you," said Jeff. "I've had enough."

The fist came down again.

"Okay, okay," Jeff said. "I'll have some ice cream."

The desserts were ordered. As we ate, the music from the festival party, supplied by a local punk band, was getting louder.

Pike's expression softened and she started nodding her head to the beat. She very carefully took a wallet from her handbag and gently placed our sketches in it. She suddenly looked at me, smiling beatifically.

CRASH!

"I HAVE SOMETHING TO SAY!" her husband shouted, breathing hard and visibly fuming.

"We go to the party. NOW!"

"Just a minute," says Jeff. "You told us to order a dessert and I'm still eating it."

I thought the guy was going to explode. Instead he folded his arms and glared at Jeff, willing him to eat faster.

Pike took two creased photographs of a boy and a girl from her wallet and laid them on the table.

"These are my children," she said, suddenly sad.

The last spoonful of ice cream was sliding into Jeff's mouth as the massive fist came down heavier and louder than before, shaking the room.

"WE–GO–NOW!!"

Everybody else shot from their seats and scurried to the door, with the exception of Pike, who grabbed my arm and yanked me down, slamming me back into my chair.

"YOU! Stay here!" she snapped.

The room had emptied apart from Pike, me and the councillor. He slowly stalked around the table, past us and to the door, staring at us all the while. At the doorway he paused and gave us a long, meaningful glare before leaving and slamming the door loudly behind him.

Pike was still holding my arm in a grip of iron. I opted to perform my critically well-received impersonation of a rabbit caught in headlights.

"Do you know…" she intoned, "…he…is the most…jealous man…in the WORLD!"

I immediately had a vision of the lunatic pulling a revolver from his car's glove compartment, cocking the trigger and stumbling back towards the building in the moonlight, drawn by Frank Miller.

"Oh…really? Er…" I quipped.

"Do you know…" she continued in the same monotone, "…that we have been…divorced for five years…but he still won't allow me to look at…another MAN?"

As she said "MAN" her hand fell from my arm and slapped onto my thigh, grabbing it in that same iron grip, just as the door burst open and her furious ex-husband stormed back in.

"YOU–GO–NOW!!"

He didn't have to tell me twice. I was out of the chair, iron grip or no, and out of that door faster than a preacher's prick up a cow's ass.

In the bar I joined Jeff, Vijaya, Anders and Ilpo who were in the middle of plotting how to spring me from the dining room.

Relaxing now in the large crowded bar, we stayed for a few more hours, chatting and drinking beer. Every now and again, Pike would come up behind me, ruffle my hair and ask me to dance.

"Sorry. I can't dance." I'd repeat and stay put.

Occasionally the dark form of her ex-husband would loom through the crowd, glower at me briefly, then stride off. When we left for the hotel at around two in the morning Pike was still going strong, pogoing with the punks.

The mayor did eventually turn up at the party closing the festival on the next afternoon, in the park where Kemi stages the building of the biggest ice castle in the world every year. The castle has a pub, restaurants with tables of ice and even a chapel where marriages take place.

After the party, everybody went to–where else?–the municipal sauna in the park where Jeff, Anders and I were squashed together nude with a couple of dozen Finns in a sauna built for ten. One wiry old reprobate, an aged Finnish comic artist, stood up and raised his bottle.

"This is what life's all about!" he proclaimed. **Beer! Sauna! Naked men!"**

––––––––––––

The truth is, all of these con stories pale into insignificance when compared to the most extravagantly outrageous and unbelievably shocking event in the history of comic festivals, one that made Spanish national newspaper headlines. Steel yourself. This really did happen.

In 2002, the seventh annual comic festival in the picturesque southern Spanish city of Granada was awash with controversy. The local politicians in charge of funding the event had been increasingly reticent about coughing up cash and had left it right up to the last minute before approving funds, even though the festival had been steadily growing in stature every year. This resulted in several planned guests and events being cancelled. It seemed to be increasingly apparent that this would be the final show and the organisers were distinctly unhappy about the situation and the behaviour of the politicians. The founder and director of the festival, Alejandro Casasola, was furious about the way they'd buggered him around for a year and was now facing the end of his dream. All his hard work had come to nothing.

On the last night of the free festival, which attracted fifty thousand attendees, the expensive and glamorous award ceremony took place, honouring the guests and paying tribute to the politicians who had provided the funding. Held in a packed auditorium overlooking the famous Alhambra castle, the ceremony began normally enough, with the emcee opening the proceedings and cracking jokes about the Spanish comic industry to good-humoured applause and laughter. Alejandro Casasola joined him on stage and presented his formal appreciation of the funds supplied by the city council and a local youth group and spoke of the cultural value of the festival to the area. The master of ceremonies then returned to the podium and began to announce the start of the comic awards when all hell broke loose.

Suddenly the air was rent with deafening automatic weapon fire as a dozen men dressed as Afghan terrorists and a woman wearing a full head-to-toe burka spilled onto the stage, shouting and swearing angrily in Spanish and shooting their kalashnikovs into the air. Led by what appeared to be Osama bin Laden, they grabbed the emcee, stripped him to his underpants and strapped a bomb to his chest. Audience members screamed, some fleeing the auditorium while others excitedly jumped up and down, cheering and snapping photos as it quickly became apparent to them that this was some kind of extravagant stunt.

Even though it was a staged performance it remained a shocking spectacle, the shouts and constant eardrum-rattling gunfire striking genuine terror into the hearts of the audience. Demanding the list of awards, the "terrorists" read out the names of the winners, roughly dragging them one-by-one onto the stage. In the audience, next to Fantagraphics editor Eric Reynolds, Peter Bagge, the American writer and artist of *Hate*, sat there fervently hoping that he wasn't among their number.

He was. Grabbed by the lapels, he was hauled to the podium where a rocket launcher was aimed at his head and the terrorists yelled Spanish insults in his ear. The award recipients, decadent purveyors of Western cultural imperialism, were lashed together at the wrists and informed that they were all going to be shot.

By now, most realised that it was all an act but the audience watched on, open-mouthed in horror as outrage piled upon outrage. The terrorists displayed their hatred of Western culture by burning images of Ronald MacDonald, the Virgin Mary and world-famous local author Federico Garcia Lorca.

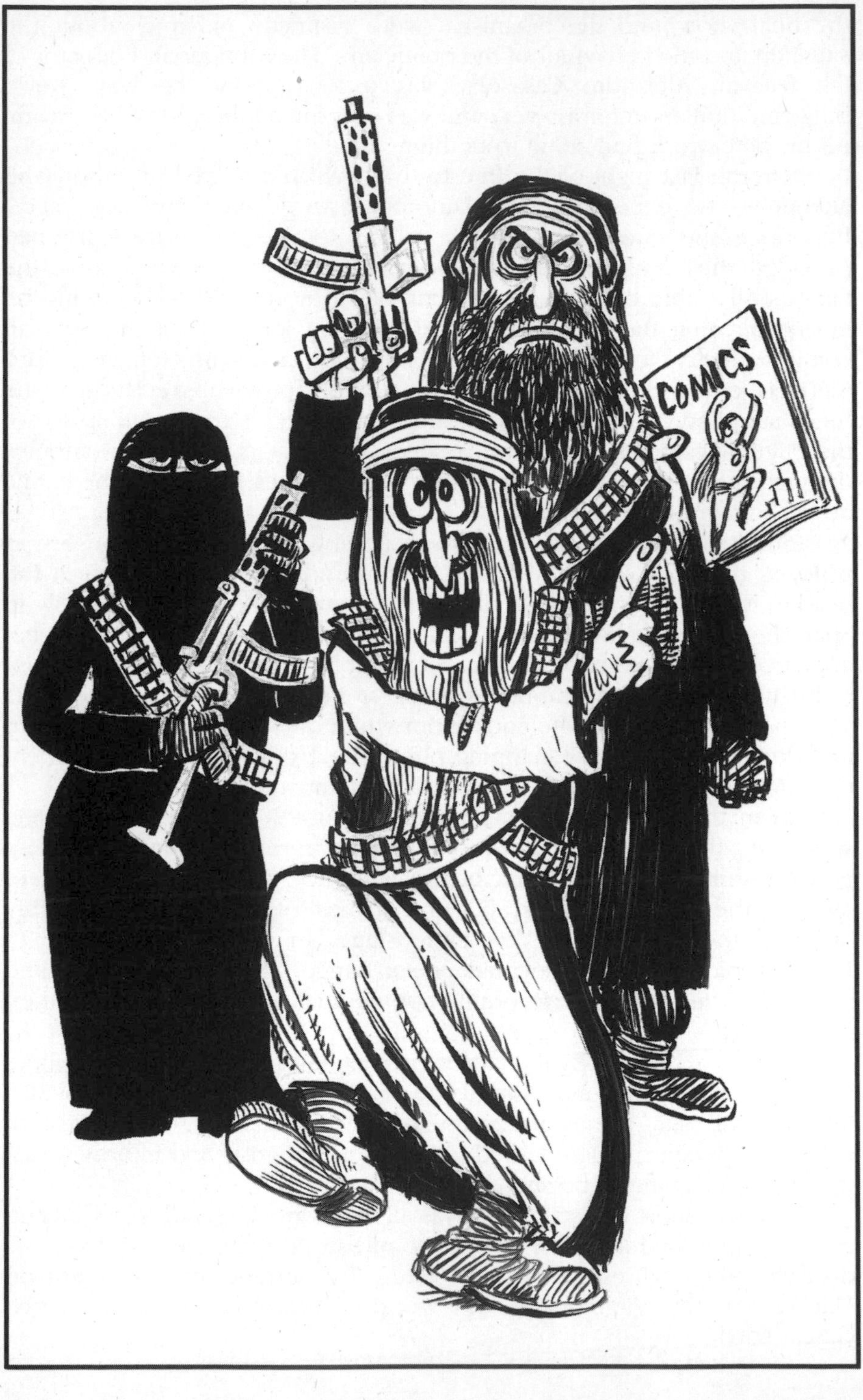
COMICS

Using the butt of his gun, one of the terrorists smashed the top off the podium, leaving two columns that bore a startling resemblance to the twin towers of the World Trade Center, destroyed only one year previously. "Osama" aimed a paper airplane at them. When it hit a column, both spectacularly burst into flames as the terrorists danced, cheered and fired into the air as the audience groaned and howled in disbelief.

Throughout this, the bin Laden character had been squatting on the floor, leafing through a pile of comic books he'd declared he was going to burn. His face radiated disgust as he flipped through their pages. However, his expression slowly changed as he intermittently stopped and appeared to read them, a smile breaking out across his face. His eyes shone and he jumped up, excited and amazed.

"Hey! These comics are great!" he shouted. "I've been wrong all along! Hooray for Western civilization! Untie these brilliant comic book people!"

The mood suddenly and drastically changed as music blared from the speakers and a chorus line of gyrating go-go dancers appeared. Center stage, the woman in the burka ripped it off, revealing herself to be completely naked, save for a pair of high-heels and long black gloves. One of the terrorists whipped open his robes and within seconds she was on her knees before him, performing an energetic blow-job. A few minutes later and they were at it like mink on heat, banging away in full view of the audience as their fellow thespians burst into song. This last act climaxed as the copulating couple did it doggy-fashion.

Peter Bagge was gobsmacked.

"It was the most mind-blowing extravaganza I've ever seen in my life!" he reported. "I hope the Eisner Award people take note!"

Alejandro Casasola, it appeared, had decided to show the politicians exactly what he thought of them and had arranged the whole spectacle, no expense spared. The event was directed by a well-known Spanish filmmaker, bin Laden and the emcee were nationally famous actors and the live-sex couple were porn stars. Seeing no possible future for the festival, Casasola had decided to go out with a bang. Literally.

Inexplicably, the festival did continue under his direction and still does so every March. •

CHAPTER TWO

SIGN OF A GOOD LAUGH

Many comic creators spend a considerable amount of time each year going to conventions or festivals and doing signings for comic stores and, as a result, spend bags of time with people they've never met before.

Daniel Clowes, creator of *Eightball*, actually met his wife at a signing. She had absolutely no interest whatsoever in comics and was only there to get her boyfriend's copies signed as he had to go to work. SF writer Harlan Ellison also met *his* wife at a signing in Liverpool. She worked in the comic store.

Signings at comic stores are notoriously unpredictable. The renowned Gilbert Shelton once did a London shop and not one punter turned up. Unsurprisingly, the turnouts are usually directly related to the amount of advance advertising of the event by the store. Some blasé retailers think it's enough to stick a few fliers on the counter and can't understand it when only a few fans turn up.

I've found that most proprietors and their staff are friendly and fun and a good time is had by all at the after-signing dinner or pub, though occasionally you'll come across a real cold fish. After signing at one store, the owner sullenly drove me to my signing at his other shop, a one-hour journey that seemed to take forever, saying little but how much he hated comics and how he was only in it for the money.

A few retailers simply don't see the reality of what it means for us to do a signing, namely the loss of a day or two's income in order to promote our work and their store. The events can be quite draining, sometimes chatting, signing and providing free sketches to a long line of customers for two or three hours or more.

Invariably I don't get a fee but *do* expect the travelling expenses to be met, food and drink after the signing and a hotel room covered if I have to stop the night. Fortunately most are happy to fork out, as Stephen Holland of Nottingham's *Page 45* put it, "To say thank you to the creators for producing the books that make our living and to say thank you to our customers for supporting us".

I always stipulate that I must be taken for a meal at a restaurant or at least a pub with good food. This dates back to a signing I did about fifteen years ago when, after a three hour signing, I was taken to the owners' dingy flat to be treated to a bowl of tasteless brown rice gloop–and no wine! I was not a happy bunny.

Similarly, it only takes one occasion of accepting a bed for the night at a retailer's apartment that's never experienced the joy of a duster or vacuum cleaner, being given a lumpy two-seater couch to sleep on and waking to find your clothes covered in cat hairs to insist on hotel or at least B&B accommodation in the future.

Previous to this, I *had* stayed at places that *were* very acceptable, though one time, in the taxi back to his place after a late night curry, Dave Holmes, the proprietor of *The Magic Labyrinth* in Leicester asked if I minded spiders.

"Aw, no, " I replied, "I live in a old house. We've lots of spiders."

"Great," he said. "I've got seventy-two tarantulas."

And he had–plus assorted scorpions and snakes. We had great fun playing with them and I still have the dried tarantula he gave me, though one of its legs has unfortunately and unaccountably dropped off inside its plastic box. He warned me to make sure my hands were well scrubbed after touching the creatures as tarantula hairs cause painful rashes and inflammation to human skin. He'd discovered this to his cost after once taking a leak without doing so and spent most of an hour shrieking and running cold water over his plonker.

The strangest thing about staying at his place was trying to get to sleep to the accompaniment of chirping crickets. His pets' food often escaped when he fed them and congregated behind the central heating radiators at night to keep warm.

———————

Neil Gaiman was doing a signing in a store in Boston, during his tenure on the highly acclaimed *Sandman*, a book that managed to cross over into the unearthly realm of non-comic readers and developed a huge cult following. As is often the case, while signing you're occasionally assessing the line of fans queuing up to get books autographed. As Neil did this, he couldn't help but be aware of a tall and incredibly beautiful young lady who he later discovered was a professional model. She got closer and closer as he worked the line until she was standing right before him. He looked up at her and she fainted on the spot. Bang. Down she went. Neil rushed from behind his table.

"Oh my God! Are you okay?"

She was and he gave her a big hug, signed her books and she went away happy.

On the *Sandman Season of Mists* tour, Neil's signing for a line of folk at a comic store when the disgruntled guy before him says, in all seriousness, "Has it ever occurred to you that the things you write about are all true?" Neil hastily changed the subject before the crackpot could begin to expound his personal belief system.

Neil's a rarity in the comics world: someone's who's got a huge comic fan base who's gone on to become a big name in prose fiction but hasn't turned his back on his comic book roots, still writing best-selling comics and occasional movies. This has given him the highest profile of any single comic writer, a superstar status. At cons like San Diego, he's restricted to entering by a back door, doing a panel and exiting fast before he's besieged by a thousand fans. The words of Alan Moore, as related in the last chapter, have come back to haunt him.

Last year he's invited to the Philippines for a signing. Leaving the hotel, he heads out to the venue, a large tent-like structure. Entering by the back, he finds himself on a stage and confronted by three thousand screaming Philippinos who are, apparently, the loudest people on the planet. His first thought is that he's wandered onto the stage of a rock concert by mistake and makes to retreat. Nope. This is it, he's told as he's pushed back on.

The signing started at 4.00pm and finished at around 1.00am the following morning and there were still people waiting.

This is all a little different from when Neil first impinged upon the world of comics. One of his first prose books, *Don't Panic–The Official Guide to The Hitch-Hiker's Guide to the Galaxy* was released in 1988. He'd already started writing his first comic series for DC, *Black Orchid*, and was in New York to visit them when he received a message from *Don't Panic* publisher Simon and Schuster, asking him to pop into the *Forbidden Planet* store to sign the stock they had.

Entering the store, he approached the counter.

"Hi, I'm Neil Gaiman," he said to the large surly sales clerk.

"Gimme yer bag!" he snarled.

Neil obediently handed it over.

"Whaddya wan'?"

"Er, I'm here to sign your copies of *Don't Panic*," said Neil.

"We ain't got any."

"There are some over there," said Neil, pointing to a display and dump bin containing about twenty-five copies.

The guy rolled his eyes, heaved himself out of his chair and slowly lumbered over to the bin, as pissed-off as can be. Snatching up three copies, he trundled back and violently slammed them down on the counter. Neil took out his pen and signed them.

"Okay? You satisfied now?" sneered the clerk.

"Can I have my bag back?" said Neil.

Following his rise to comic fame, Neil received repeated requests from the store but refused to sign there again until it changed hands a few years later.

There's an apocryphal story of how Neil, having written the first few issues of *Sandman*, walks into a New York comic store and, seeing copies in stock, promptly signs them all. Seeing him, the outraged proprietor makes him buy all the ones he's "defaced". Neil was delighted to hear this tale and thinks that it perhaps evolved from the previous one.

Dave Gibbons first learned that you sometimes have to be very careful what you say at a signing during the first US *Watchmen* tour. Signing at a con in Atlanta for a large queue, Dave was chatting away to the punters crowding round, answering the multitude of questions they had about the innovative new book, one that would drastically influence the superhero genre and make him and Alan Moore comic superstars.

"It's a very bleak vision of America," a fan says.

"Oh, it could be worse," quips Dave. "At least you win the Vietnam War this time!"

There's a bit of chuckling that stops abruptly when a heavily tattooed biker leans his elbow on Dave's table.

"So you think Vietnam's funny, huh?"

A terrible hush descends as Dave stares up at the menacing Vietnam vet towering over him.

"Obviously, it isn't funny," Dave states. "We respect what you went through."

This defused the situation but made Dave all too aware that in other peoples' countries there are different sensibilities that you have to take into account.

Dave first met *Eddy Current* artist Ted McKeever at this same signing and afterwards they went for a few drinks. Probably most famous for his *X-Men* work, writer Chris Claremont later arrived at the bar and joined them, apparently plonking himself down without invitation and horning in on their conversation. Dave and Ted had a few more beers before heading off to eat. It was only later that Dave realised that they'd left Chris to pay the whole night's bar tab. I must point out that, in the UK, we don't have bar tabs. In pubs, you pay as you go–before each drink.

Sometimes at store signings you're confronted with reporters from the local newspaper waiting to interview you, especially if it's in a quiet rural town where the inhabitants still point at passing airplanes and the reporter is desperate for a news item marginally more exciting than "Local Man Slips on Banana Skin". British provincial newspapers do have their own agenda, namely that if it's nothing to do with the town, it's not newsworthy.

My favorite local paper story is that of the *Accrington Observer* from 1912. When the *Titanic* sank there was nothing on the front page, nor the next. A tiny column on page three was headlined "Accrington Man Dies in Sea Disaster". Perfectly true.

The number of times I've seen the inevitably factually dubious article containing the interview I've done while at a comic store titled "The Life of Bryan" is legion. *The Killing Joke* and DC cover artist Brian Bolland always gets, of course, "The Life of Brian". And they all must think that they're being so witty and original.

When *The Tale of One Bad Rat* came out in 1994 I did a signing at the *Waterstones* bookstore in Preston and was interviewed by the local paper. The article that subsequently appeared in *The Lancashire Evening Post* was actually quite good and seriously dealt with book's subject, namely that of the psychological after-effects of child sexual abuse. Unfortunately, the sub-editor whose job it had been to go through and write all the headlines must have done it in a hurry. The clod had obviously only scanned the first paragraph relating that a *COMIC* artist had done a *SIGNING* and sensitively titled this discussion of child abuse "Sign of a Good Laugh".

In the eighties, the proprietor of a certain Scottish comic and SF store was busted for possession of a tiny amount of grass in his home village of Biggar. Yes, that's its name. At his trial, he came up before a local magistrate who was a well-known eccentric. The previous week he'd ordered the overweight defendant to return for trial in a month, threatening him with a fine if he hadn't lost at least eight pounds by then. On hearing the retailer's case, he condemned him to write a ten-page dissertation on the dangers of drugs. That really was the sentence. The local paper ran with the story, its front-page headline proclaiming "Biggar Man Gets Essay".

But, yes, to rein in my demented ramblings, and return to what I'm supposed to be actually talking about, you *do* have to be careful sometimes in accepting an invitation.

In the mid-eighties, Colin Upton went to a convention in Victoria in British Columbia. Arriving the night before, he disembarked from the ferry from his hometown of Vancouver and made his way to the comic store hosting the event. Once there, the owner reneged on his promise to provide him with a room for the night, claiming that he'd no idea what Colin was doing there at all. Colin ended up staying awake all night, roaming the November streets of Victoria, shivering in the cold and drizzle until he eventually stumbled upon a twenty-four hour diner where he stayed till early morning, drying off and drinking hot tea. Naturally, he never dealt with the store again.

———

One time at the San Diego Comicon, the illustrious French comic artist Jean Giraud, aka *Moebius*, was approached by a small group of fans who offered to take him out to dinner. They had a store that they'd very much like to show him and there was a top quality Italian restaurant just round the corner. Not having anything planned, Moebius agreed on impulse and they met him around six outside the convention center.

A beat-up old van pulled up, driven by a friend of theirs who was headed their way, and they all piled in. This should have been the first warning sign but it was too late by now: he'd agreed to go and off they set. The conversation in the van was a little strained, not least because the journey seemed interminable. Moebius kept being told that they'd be arriving shortly but it was over two hours later before they finally pulled up in an unremarkable town in the middle of nowhere.

Okay, so they're dropped off outside the store and their driver zooms off back home to another town. The store is a disappointment, to say the least: more like a corridor, stacked with second hand comics. Ah well, off to the restaurant. At least there's a good meal waiting. And there is. The trattoria is a top-notch establishment and the food and wine are excellent. After a few litres of wine, a couple of the guys are quite tanked. At the end of the meal, the retailer's mates head off for some bar, leaving him and Moebius chatting over their coffee.

When the bill arrives, the guy's jaw drops. He gulps and frantically searches his pockets, unearthing a ten dollar bill which he places it on the table, utterly shamefaced. He's totally broke and, a little drunk, forgot to ask his pals for the cash they promised in return for having dinner with the great man. This is in the days before mobile phones were common-place, so he can't contact them.

Moebius is not well pleased. He has to pay the hefty bill with his own credit card and then shell out for the two-hour taxi drive back to San Diego. There's a moral in here somewhere.

Moebius, one of my favorite all-time comic artists, is quite well known for, to put it kindly, being on a higher mental plane than most other mortals otherwise he probably would have seen the signs and declined the dinner invite. Once, Dark Horse publisher Mike Richardson spent two weeks vacation with him, driving him around Texas and Arizona, visiting Native American holy places and suchlike. Now Mike is instantaneously recognisable, anywhere. He's a giant. I'm around six foot tall and I get a crick in my neck if we're standing talking. He told me that two months after their vacation, he runs into Moebius at a comic convention.

"Hi!" says Mike, "How've you been?"

Moebius stares at him blankly and says "Who are you?"

––––––––––

During a con in Buenos Aires, Dave Gibbons, Mark Waid, *Gotham Knights* writer Devin Grayson and Spanish artist Carlos Pacheco and his wife were approached by some fans connected to the organization of the event.

"As a token of our regard, we want to make for you a traditional Argentinean barbeque."

They unanimously accepted and were met at around eight in the evening at their hotel and driven off in a motley collection of battered cars to their promised banquet. Over an hour and a half later, they arrived at a grim complex of suburban apartment blocks and were deposited in a communal garden littered with rusting prams and car wrecks.

"Now you are here, we can start!" they were informed.

Dave asked where the toilet was.

"Oh, go up those stairs to the fourth floor," one of the fans said. "Knock on the door of number forty-nine and my auntie will let you use hers."

The guests were supplied with a collection of bottles of wine and beer and waited while the fans built the barbie. By this time it was ready to start cooking it was around eleven.

The food was eventually served at twelve-thirty and consisted solely of huge hunks of burnt meat. No bread, salad, chips or dips, just burnt meat.

The fans were so amiable and eager to please, the invitees just didn't have the heart to complain. They were eventually ferried back to their hotel about four in the morning.

Yes, inevitably things can go somewhat awry during signings, cons or tours. As part of the *Luther Arkwright* tour in the eighties, I did signings in Belfast and Dublin. This was still during *The Troubles* before the *Good Friday Agreement* and I was only the second comic creator to sign in Ireland, the first being illustrator John Bolton.

So I'm met at Belfast airport by Paul Trimble, the proprietor of *Thunder Road Comics*, and we drive into the city. I'm quite unnerved at the sight of passing armoured transports and squaddies who look like they aren't old enough to shave pointing machine guns straight at my chest but Paul doesn't seem to notice them and is chatting merrily away about the signing and his store.

"…Oh yes," he continues, "and we've filled the window with your posters."

Posters? I wonder.

"Which posters?"

"You know," he says, "the Luther Arkwright ones."

"What? The large prints of the cover of Volume Two? The ones where he's draped in a bloody big Union Jack?"

"Don't worry!" Paul laughs. "If anyone tries to shoot you we'll throw ourselves in front of the bullets!"

I think this was intended to reassure me.

As it turned out, the signing was very successful and lasted about four hours, people coming from all over Northern Ireland. Today fans are a lot more blasé about such events over there. Paul's store was on the second floor of an 18th century house. Halfway through the session, the people from the store below ran upstairs, terrified and shouting to the fans to move back. There were so many people in the room that the floor was actually bulging downwards, the beams bending and the ceiling plaster cracking, threatening to imminently collapse.

Next day I was taken to the railway station and put on a train bound for Dublin. The journey was disrupted because of a bomb threat against it. The train was stopped and the passengers had to file off and wait for the couple of coaches which ferried us through *Bandit Country*–the border area between Northern Ireland and Eire–and through the frighteningly beweaponed army checkpoint to a station on the other side of the border where we were put on an Irish Republic train to continue our journey.

This time I found myself sitting across from a middle-aged American couple. They were doing Europe at the rate of one or two countries a day and now it was Eire's turn. When I asked them where they were from, they boasted proudly "We're from Kentucky! We're *WASPS!*"

_____

The preceding was just to set the scene, because here's the story right now. Let it be a lesson to you.

Okay, I arrive at Dublin and am met at the station by a lovely young lady whose name I can't remember but I'll call her Kerry. We take a cab over to the bed and breakfast place that Kerry's employer, Forbidden Planet, has booked for me. I quickly drop off my travelling bag, jump back into the waiting taxi and we drive to the city center. It's the first time I've been there, so I'm trying to rubberneck as I chat with Kerry. We enter a large square and she points out the famous *Royal College of Surgeons* building.

After lunch and a few glasses of rather nice wine, we walk around the corner to Forbidden Planet and I meet the manager. The signing isn't for another couple of hours so we take off again, taking another cab to the church of St Michan's.

There's a scribbled note of visiting times pinned up on the notice board inside the porch and we wait for the next one. About ten minutes later, the sexton, breath heavy with beer, returns from the pub. We pay him fifty pence each and he gives us the guided tour.

The church itself is interesting enough–the stained glass inspired by *The Book of Kells*, the organ on which Handel composed the *Messiah* and so forth–but it's the crypts below that contain the reason for our visit. The dark, dusty and cobwebbed medieval crypts, cluttered with piles of coffins, have a peculiar feature: the atmosphere down there mummifies the bodies. The sexton shows off three for our delectation. They are, supposedly, a knight, a nun and a thief who's been punished by having his feet and hands chopped off. The mummies' skin is like old blackened leather, their fingernails long. It was this place that first inspired M.R. James to write ghost stories and these stiffs crop up in his tales again and again in one form or another.

Anyhow, back in the sunshine, we ride back into town and kill the rest of the time before the signing by strolling around the center. Dublin has three statues there, pretty close to each other. One is of *Molly Malone* and her wheelbarrow, another is a modern art sculpture of some sort of water nymph in a fountain and the other is a column topped by a statue of a Victorian worthy leaning on his cane. They're known locally as *The Tart with the Cart, The Floozie in the Jacuzzi* and *The Dick with the Stick*.

This time the signing is three and a half hours of doing free sketches, chatting to the fans and, well, signing books. It finishes around half past six at which point Kerry takes me to the neighbouring pub for a pint of Guinness while the manager coppers up. The Guinness in Dublin tastes beautiful. It makes Guinness I've had just about anywhere else taste positively mediocre. It goes down like mother's milk. The manager joins us for another pint, then has to leave, handing Kerry some cash to cover my dining and drinking expenses. Yes, being a comic artist is a tough job but someone has to do it.

A couple of pints later and Kerry suggests that we go to eat and then meet up with some of her mates. We have spaghetti and a bottle of red wine at an Italian place, then meet her friends at a noisy and crowded pub. They turn out to be punks–mohican haircuts, the works–but are very amiable and seem to have an endless supply of jokes and movie star impersonations, the best of which is Sean Connery. We have a couple more pints of Guinness.

About half past midnight, Kerry takes us back to Forbidden Planet where, using her staff key, she lets us in and we go to the back room. This was apparently a regular thing with them–somewhere in the city center they could go to in-between pubs to have a sneaky spliff. After a few joints and starting to feel the worse for wear, I remember that I have to be up around six thirty that morning to get my flight back to England.

As we exit FP, Kerry and the punks urge me to come along with them to a night club–it's a *Sex Pistols* theme night–but I'm eminently sensible and insist that I have to leave.

"No problem," says Kerry, "You see down there, at the end of the street? That's the big square with the College of Surgeons. Just go to the far side and there's a large taxi rank."

We say our goodbyes and I walk off, turning to wave them fondly goodbye when I reach the square. They wave back and head off down a side street.

I cross the square thinking what a wonderful city Dublin is. Such friendly people. And what a nice tree-lined square. And there's the taxi rank with lots of waiting cabs.

It's only as I approach the cars that, with a sinking feeling, I suddenly realize that I've no idea of the name of the bed and breakfast joint nor its location. What a bugger! My bag's there, with my cheque-book, passport and tickets. I try to think of its name but I don't think I even noticed, I was in and out of there so quickly. I don't even have the home number of the FP manager.

I walk back down the square to the row of telephone kiosks I passed. Perhaps if I look down the list of guesthouses in the yellow pages I'll recognize the name of my bed and breakfast. Oh. No phone books. Hmm. I make a vain attempt at trying to dial directory enquiries, with the ludicrous assumption that I may be able to get an operator to kindly read me the list of city guesthouses. A silly idea, made logical by drink, but I can't get through anyway. What to do?

Thinking back to the taxi ride here, I try to remember any landmarks. I remember a large hotel, but not its name. The B&B itself was just one of a long terrace of nondescript four floor houses. But I *do* remember which road we entered the square from so I determine to follow it, setting off at a brisk pace.

I later found out that, because of Dublin's Byzantine one-way system, I was walking in exactly the opposite direction I should have been heading in.

It's not very long before I'm passed by an officer of the *Garda*–the Irish police–on a motorbike. He pulls over a little in front of me and crosses the road to scope out some shops. I presume that he's seen something suspicious but, no, he's at the window of a travel agency, checking out the cheap holiday offers. He actually jumps when I pipe up from behind him.

"Er, excuse me…"

I didn't know what to expect from a copper being approached by a drunken foreigner on a dark street in the middle of the night but he's even-tempered and unexpectedly polite. I explain the situation as best I can in my inebriated state.

After he's asked all the obvious questions he adds "…and this hotel you noticed–can you remember its name?"

"No," I reply, "it was sort of a big motel with a big neon sign and it's name wasn't Irish sounding. That's it: it sounded very English."

"Was it *The Buckingham*?"

"By God, yes it was!"

I thank him profusely and head back to the taxi rank. I figure that I'll go to the Buckingham and then walk around looking for B&Bs.

I didn't have to. As the cab approached the motel I happened to look out of the side window and, amazingly, recognised the wrought ironwork in the guesthouse's front door window, something I'd entirely forgotten.

Ever since this occasion, on arrival at a hotel or B&B, the first thing that I do is grab a couple of their business cards and stash them in different pockets. If you learn anything from this tale, take my advice and do the same.

Strangehaven writer, artist and self-publisher Gary Spencer Millidge was invited to the Amadora Festival in 2005 and duly drove to London's delightful Gatwick Airport to take the plane to Lisbon. After a few very pleasant days of comics, sightseeing, wining and dining (to which I can attest, having also been there that year) he was ferried to the airport on the last night in time to catch his return flight. It wasn't until he was through passport control and was looking for his plane back to Gatwick on the monitor that he discovered that the flight number on his e-ticket was one for a flight to London's equally delightful Heathrow Airport. A mistake had been made when his publisher booked his flight and he was returning to a London airport that was thirty miles as the crow flies away from the airport where his car was parked. Too late to get another flight, he took it, and, too late to catch a train or bus at the other end, he had to fork out a hundred and twenty quid for a taxi to Gatwick.

––––––––––

Dutch cartoonist Frans Mensink is an adventurous type. He has a World War One *Sopwith Camel* biplane and flies it around the skies over Holland. In the nineties, he receives an invitation to be a guest at an obscure Russian small press comic con, one that can't afford to offer travelling expenses. He thanks them for the invite but cries off. They continue to invite him annually for several years and each time he politely declines but always sends them a piece of artwork for their exhibition. One year, on impulse, he thinks "Why the hell not?" and accepts.

After changing planes at Moscow, he arrives at a tiny airport in the back of beyond in the middle of a Russian Winter, the sort that Napoleon and Hitler had so much fun with. He's dismayed, however, to find no one there to meet him. A blizzard is raging outside, so he hangs around for several hours hoping that someone from the con will turn up. Nobody does.

After much asking around he finds a lorry driver who can speak no Dutch or English but who's headed in the direction of the village where the con is being held.

They step out into the cold. It's bloody freezing. Once in the cab of the truck, the driver pulls out a pot of what looks disturbingly like axle grease and liberally plasters it over Frans' shocked face before doing the same thing to himself. Frans realises that this must be to protect them from the sub-zero temperatures.

They drive for several hours through the unrelenting snowstorm. There's no conversation and Frans eventually drifts off to sleep. He's rudely awaked as the lorry pulls to a shuddering halt and the driver jabbers at him in Russian while indicating the side window of the cab. Rubbing the ice off its interior, Frans can make out some faint lights twinkling through the gusting snow. The driver grunts, indicating that this is where they must part company. Frans thanks him and climbs down to the road. The lorry coughs into life again and bounces off down the pot-holed highway into the blizzard, leaving Frans standing in the biting cold, blinking through watering eyes at the lights, visible in the far distance over snowbound fields.

Pulling spare clothing out of his bag, he wraps it around his head and shoulders, it being too cold to remove his coat, and heads off in the direction of the village. Struggling through waist-high snowdrifts, he's

getting colder and increasingly terrified, as the lights seem to recede before him.

After what seems like an eternity he arrives, exhausted, at a tiny hamlet. He's sodden and numb and his teeth are chattering uncontrollably. The place looks like a set from a Universal *Frankenstein* Christmas movie with a few lights flickering in some of the windows but no other signs of intelligent life. Looking around, he sees a barn-like structure that he assumes to be the village hall. He tries the door and it swings open, revealing a dark and empty entrance chamber. Then Frans notices a light, coming through the door at the end of a corridor and heads on over to it. Swathed in dripping, icy clothes and with his face covered in dirty grease he stumbles into a large hall.

A couple of dozen folk, huddled around a large brazier in the center of the hall look up at him in horror as he starts babbling at them, trying to explain what the hell he's doing there. They gape at him in awe as he sweeps his eyes around the assembly, desperately searching for a glimmer of comprehension. There isn't one.

Suddenly he notices that the walls have sheets of paper pinned on them–artwork! Comic artwork! And some of them are by him! Running over to one of them, he points at it and gestures at himself.

"I did this!" he shouts.

The group bursts into an amazed frenzy as they realise who he is. He's the first guest they've invited that's actually turned up!

Frans is immediately warmly welcomed and seated near the fire to dry off. He's presented with a large pot of roubles that's been building up over the years as a guest fund. It's not a fortune but it's enough to supply everybody with vodka as they embark on a three-day binge party, complete with balalaikas and much singing, before his hosts put him on the plane back home.

A few years ago superhero comic writer Mark Waid of *Kingdom Come* fame was invited to a convention in New England. He received his airline tickets, duly took the plane and, as is usual, was met at the airport by two convention people and driven to his hotel room. All as you would expect, except...there was no convention! These two fanboys had forked out the price of the flight and hotel just so that they could hang out with their favorite writer all weekend. Bet it was fun.

Something similar happened to me in the early eighties. Veteran comic artist Arthur (*Buttonman*) Ranson and I were invited to the

Chaumont-Gistoux Comics Festival, held in a tiny village outside Brussels. Mary decided to join us. The arrangements were very, very last minute and we ended up paying for the flight up front, as did Arthur, whom we met at Brussels airport.

Eventually two guys came to collect us and drove us to the old *auberge* in the village where we had rooms, explaining that the festival began next morning–and so it did.

The "festival" consisted of a small exhibition of framed comic artwork in one of the back rooms of the auberge and a table in the garden topped with a few second hand comic albums for sale. The artwork and books belonged to one of the guys who became identified as the organizer. The other guy, whose name was Dan, only vaguely knew him but had been roped in as the "festival driver" as he was a comic fan and lived locally.

During the morning, more comic artists arrived, a mixture of French and Belgians, until there were eight or nine creators and their wives. And that was it. This guy had organized the "event" just so that he could spend three days with us.

And, *en effet*, it was very pleasant. Each day we had a large French lunch, home cooked in the auberge, and we chatted, sometimes going for a walk in the mid-afternoon sunshine.

I already knew Arthur but I'd never heard of any of the other artists and can only now remember one, Gine, who did a series of albums documenting the adventures of *Capitane Sabre*. For two nights we ate in the auberge restaurant, with its large wood fire with great hunks of Aberdeen Angus sizzling on the grill and its stone flagged floor that would often have a chicken or two strutting about or the bulldog puppy Winston (named after Churchill) urinating on it.

One night Dan and his wife Giselle took us into Brussells for a meal of *steak du cheval*–horse steak–in a restaurant in the old quarter just off *La Grande Place*. We got on really well with Dan, whom we later discovered had paid for the petrol expenses and our meal in Brussells out of his own pocket.

After we got home we weren't surprised when the organizer never refunded our or Arthur's airfare but we didn't really mind: we'd had a cool time and made a couple of friends. Dan and Gi visited us in England a few years later and we returned to see them about ten years after the "festival" and ate at the auberge again.

You may think that fake cons are strange, but what about fake artists?

In the 1980s, legendary underground cartoonist S. Clay Wilson phoned *Lambiek*, a comic store in the center of Amsterdam that has a special interest in underground comics and asked them if they'd be interested in him coming over from America to do a signing. Hell, yes they would. They paid for his flight and hotel room for a week in which he was hosted and toasted and kept supplied with high-grade dope.

Everyone thought what a great guy he was–this star of the US underground who was happy and willing to spend a week with his fans, eatin', drinkin', smokin' and reminiscin' about the good old days of *Zap Comix* and hangin' out with the likes of Robert Crumb and Gilbert Shelton.

That is, until a while after he'd departed, when the store received another phone call. This time it was from the *real* S, Clay Wilson, who'd heard that he had apparently just been in Amsterdam.

———————

This also happened to the famous superhero comic artist John Byrne who heard that he'd recently done a signing at a store in Texas when, in fact, he'd done no such thing. Contacting the store, he discovered that someone claiming to be him had phoned them and offered to do a signing. The guy's travel and luxury hotel expenses were covered and he received a hefty fee to boot. He was given a large bagful of freebie books, comics and toys from the store and was treated to a meal at an expensive restaurant afterwards.

In both of the above stories, I've never heard an explanation of how these phonies could get away without drawing sketches. Perhaps they'd learnt to copy the artists' styles? John Byrne, by the way, allegedly has a habit of carefully cleaning his hands with a fresh *Wet Wipe* after shaking hands with each fan at a signing.

———————

Diane Duane, a science fiction author who also wrote a few *Star Trek* comics and the first Trek hardcover novel, *Spock's World*, had a serial impersonator. For about a year, a woman claiming to be her would turn up at Trekkie and SF cons and be paid appearance fees to do signings and participate in panel discussions. Diane only discovered this when she attended a convention and turned up to do a signing.

A fan stepped from the crowd and declared "You ain't Diane Duane!"

Apparently the fan had been entertained by the fake one at a pre-vious con. Diane went on to spend a lot of time and trouble tracking down the impostor, who was caught, tried, convicted of fraud and, last I heard, still languishing in prison.

To return to Amsterdam and underground comics, in the eighties the creator of *The Fabulous Furry Freak Brothers*, Gilbert Shelton, and Paul Mavrides, then artist on the book, were invited over to judge, of all things, the annual *Marijuana Cultivators Competition*. Over the weekend of the event, they had to decide which was the winning weed out of a selection of twenty bags of the stuff. How their critical faculties remained intact after the first bag or two of high-grade grass I've really no idea.

On the final evening they go out to dinner with five sample bags remaining to be assessed and time fast running out. In the crowded restaurant, Gilbert has an idea and beckons the waiter over.

"Er, excuse me," he whispers, "do you think anyone here will mind if we smoke some marijuana?"

"I don't know," the waiter replies and does an about-face.

"DOES ANYBODY MIND IF THESE PEOPLE SMOKE MARIJUANA?" he bellows to the whole restaurant.

Apparently nobody did, so they managed to successfully judge the last five bags' worth. •

CHAPTER THREE

BASE FANS

Contrary to popular perception influenced, as it is, by TV and movie stereotypes, not all comic readers are drooling imbeciles with eating disorders and no sex life. After years of meeting them at cons many fans become old friends of pros and sometimes even comic pros themselves. The vast majority of fans are nice, sane, ordinary folk but there's always bound to be some that are congenitally daft, downright obnoxious, creepily odd, or undeniably crackers.

One guy phoned *Astro City* and *Marvels* writer Kurt Busiek in the middle of the night just to say how great it was that Kurt had made a criminal posing as a superhero in *Power Man and Iron Fist* come from West Monroe in Louisiana. The fan himself came from Monroe, Louisiana and was overjoyed that even a writer living way up there on the East Coast knew that all the citizens of West Monroe were total and utterly irredeemable degenerates. In reality, Kurt used West Monroe as a friend of his lived there. After this incident, Kurt had his phone number unlisted.

Watchmen colourist and artist of *World Without End*, John Higgins, was standing around in the UKCAC foyer one year, chatting with Dave Gibbons and *2000AD* and *Legion of Superheroes* artist Barry Kitson before they headed off to the hotel bar. Suddenly John was grabbed by the shoulders and forcibly turned around by a large guy whom he didn't recognize. Without introducing himself or even apologizing, he peered at John's con ID badge and turned to the ten-year-old boy standing behind him.

"Do you want John Higgins?" he asked his son.

"Naah," the kid said, pointing at Dave, "Who's that?"

His dad checked out Dave's nametag.

"Dave Gibbons."

"Yeah, I'll have him." the brat responded, thrusting his autograph book under Dave's nose.

Recently, at the party after a particularly well-attended signing in Brighton, one fan threw up all over John Higgins's brand new trainers. He's never successfully managed to get the curry stains out. This should have been no big deal to John, as one exceptionally hot and sticky New York night he was copiously spewed over by a drunk in a crowded subway train, soaking him from his waist to his previous brand new pair of trainers.

When *Hellblazer* was first published in the late eighties, writer Jamie Delano, cover artist Dave McKean and colourist Lovern Kindzierski, who related this story, were signing copies for fans before a large poster of the first cover at the San Diego Comicon.

Suddenly a loud cry of "Oh, WOW! Hellblazer!" rang out and a bloke charged over to their table, dragging along a bunch of his friends.

"I love this! I love this!" he exclaimed, urging his pals to buy copies. As he scanned the artists' name cards, he stopped and did an astonished double-take

"Oh my GOD!" he screamed, goggling at Dave. "It's DAVE MCKEAN! Oh, *WOW*! You're the reason I buy this book, man!"

Before Dave could modestly thank him, the guy erupted into a babbling torrent of praise of the kind usually reserved for supreme deities. He burbled on, becoming ever more insistent and over-the-top, while his increasingly embarrassed friends nudged him in the ribs in a vain attempt to get him to shut the fuck up.

Dave, by now also painfully embarrassed, indicated Jamie and Lovern in a desperate bid to dilute the gushing deluge of adoration by spreading it around a little.

"See–here's Jamie Delano and Lovern Kindzierski…" he said, "…the writer and the colourist on the book."

"Hell, I've not read it!" the fan cheerfully admitted. "Fuck, no! I just cut the covers off and throw that shit away!"

The fan continued in this vein as Dave looked on open-mouthed and the guy's mates, too embarrassed to be associated with him any longer, took off.

"Look," said Dave, "you really should read it. It's very good and the book works as a whole. The cover, the writing and the interior art all work together."

"Well, *okay*," he reluctantly conceded. "I think so much of you, if you say so, I'll give it a try."

Mercifully, at this point he suddenly noticed that all his friends had deserted him and he ran off to look for them.

Hellblazer , by the way, was originally going to be titled *Hellraiser*. This is much more descriptive of the John Constantine character. DC had to change it at the last minute when the Clive Barker movie was coincidentally released just before its publication. *Hellblazer* was the nearest thing they could come up with.

———————

One time in San Diego, painter Dave Dorman, well known for his cover art and *Star Wars* illustrations, was sketching for fans and chatting with his old friend, *Capital City Distribution* veteran and *Chaos Comics* sales rep, Robert Sprenger. As they talked, Robert was leafing through Dave's portfolio, pausing to study his cover paintings for the comic adaptation of Clive Barker's *Nightbreed*. Suddenly a guy barges in between them and grabs hold of the portfolio.

"Holy shit, man!" he gasps. "This is fuckin' awesome!"

Dave ignores him and carries on sketching, while Robert grows increasingly pissed off at this fan who's so rudely interrupted their conversation. The guy just won't stop talking, jabbering on in his British accent.

"What are these paintings for?" he asks.

Wearily, Robert informs him that they are the covers for *Clive Barker's Nightbreed*.

"That's great," he says, "they're perfect."

At this point, Dave looks up at him and practically falls out of his chair. It was Clive Barker.

———————

At another SD Comicon, creator and publisher of *Too Much Coffee Man*, Shannon Wheeler was at his booth when an overweight middle-aged dude completely decked out as a Klingon started checking out his books. Shannon went into his sales pitch, telling him that, if he bought a TMCM mug, he'd get a free cup of coffee. The guy, refusing to step out of character, would only speak to him in Klingon. As Shannon struggled to communicate, the Klingon appeared to get angry and made as if he wanted to attack the artist, again staying in character as a Klingon warrior. Eventually a passer-by who, astoundingly, happened to be fluent in Klingon stopped and started translating for him. It appeared that the

Klingon was wondering whether the coffee was really strong as that was the only kind Klingons drank. He had a slurp and admitted that it was okay but not as strong as (insert Klingon word here). He bought a mug and a tee-shirt.

By the way, Too Much Coffee Man has recently been performed as an opera, receiving much critical acclaim.

Some fans can get *really* scary. Long-time superhero writer Marv Wolfman and others have even received death threats for killing off cherished comic characters.

At one convention in Philadelphia, upon seeing him enter, a disgruntled guy made a bee-line straight for Marv.

"You've completely destroyed Batman!" he declared.

He obviously hated the work that Marv had done on the book but, at this time, there were dozens of other Batman titles on sale, as Marv pointed out. It didn't matter. The "fan" got angrier and angrier, adamant that Marv had "completely destroyed Batman" and destroyed him *forever*. Marv admits that his weren't the best Batman stories ever written but they certainly weren't the worst.

The guy kept going on about the supposed destruction of the character, never saying how or why he thought this and getting increasingly infuriated all the while. Eventually Marv realised that he was on a hiding to nowhere trying to debate the issue with this moron.

"Well, I'm sorry you don't like my stories," he said and turned to talk with someone else.

Marv could sense the guy going rigid with anger. He could positively feel the fury radiating from him as he continued to stand at Marv's side, breathing heavily, waiting for him to recommence the argument.

Eventually he must have realized that Marv had no interest in reopening the debate and angrily stomped off into the crowd. Marv never saw him again.

During the height of *Watchmen* mania, Dave Gibbons was being interviewed on stage in San Diego when he noticed a smiling member of the audience trying to maintain eye contact with him. Simply imagining that here was an interested fan, Dave continued to glance at him now and again as he talked, acknowledging his appreciation of the guy's interest. Then the fan started smiling a little too disturbingly, his eyes now staring right into Dave's, commanding his attention. To his horror, Dave looked on as the fan slowly and theatrically removed his convention badge, opened the safety pin on the back and slid it right through the soft skin of his wrist, smiling all the time. Dave broke eye contact and made sure that he didn't look at him again.

———————

At a recent Bristol Comic Expo, Al Davison, writer and artist of arguably the best British graphic novel ever produced, *The Spiral Cage*, was actually stalked by a strangely smiling fan.

Al was born with Spina Bifida and is very often restricted to a wheelchair. *The Spiral Cage* is his autobiography, detailing how he managed to cure himself of many of the symptoms of the condition through a mixture of martial arts training, Tai Chi and Buddhist chanting techniques. He's currently working on the sequel, *Scar Tissue*.

So, Al's in the huge converted railway engine shed that each year houses the Expo, signing at his table when this smiling Greek guy arrives who wants to review Al's graphic novel, *The Minotaur's Tale* for a website about Greek mythology in comics. All well and good. Al thinks he's a little intense but seemingly sound and they chat for a while until Al has to leave to run a comics workshop. For the hour that Al's away, the fan returns about eight times, each time staring intensely at the table for a few minutes before disappearing again. Al's wife Maggie, running their booth, attempts to engage him in conversation but, still smiling, he leaves as soon as she starts to speak.

Al returns and so does the fan and they proceed to have what's basically the same conversation they'd had earlier, almost word-for-word.

For the rest of the day, this guy follows Al around, much too close for comfort. Every time he looks around, the creep's there behind his back. Even when Al goes for dinner with one of his students, Maggie having already left for the night, he looks up and there's the fan, standing outside the restaurant window. Staring in at him. Smiling.

Leaving the restaurant, he doggedly follows Al to a taxi rank where the student, who I'll name Fred, helps Al to pack his wheelchair into a cab. As Fred steps back from the door, the Greek fan makes a rush for it and tries to jump on board. Al pushes him back out and slams the door shut while Fred forcibly restrains the guy. The fan stops struggling at this point and simply stands there, smiling, as the taxi speeds off.

Next day, as Al and Maggie are arriving back at the con, they see him still there: smiling and standing on the exact same spot. According to Fred, the fan hadn't budged an inch after the taxi had left and was still there when Fred caught a bus nearly an hour later. For all they knew, he'd been there all night. Smiling.

At the con he stalked Al again, who this time told him to bugger off

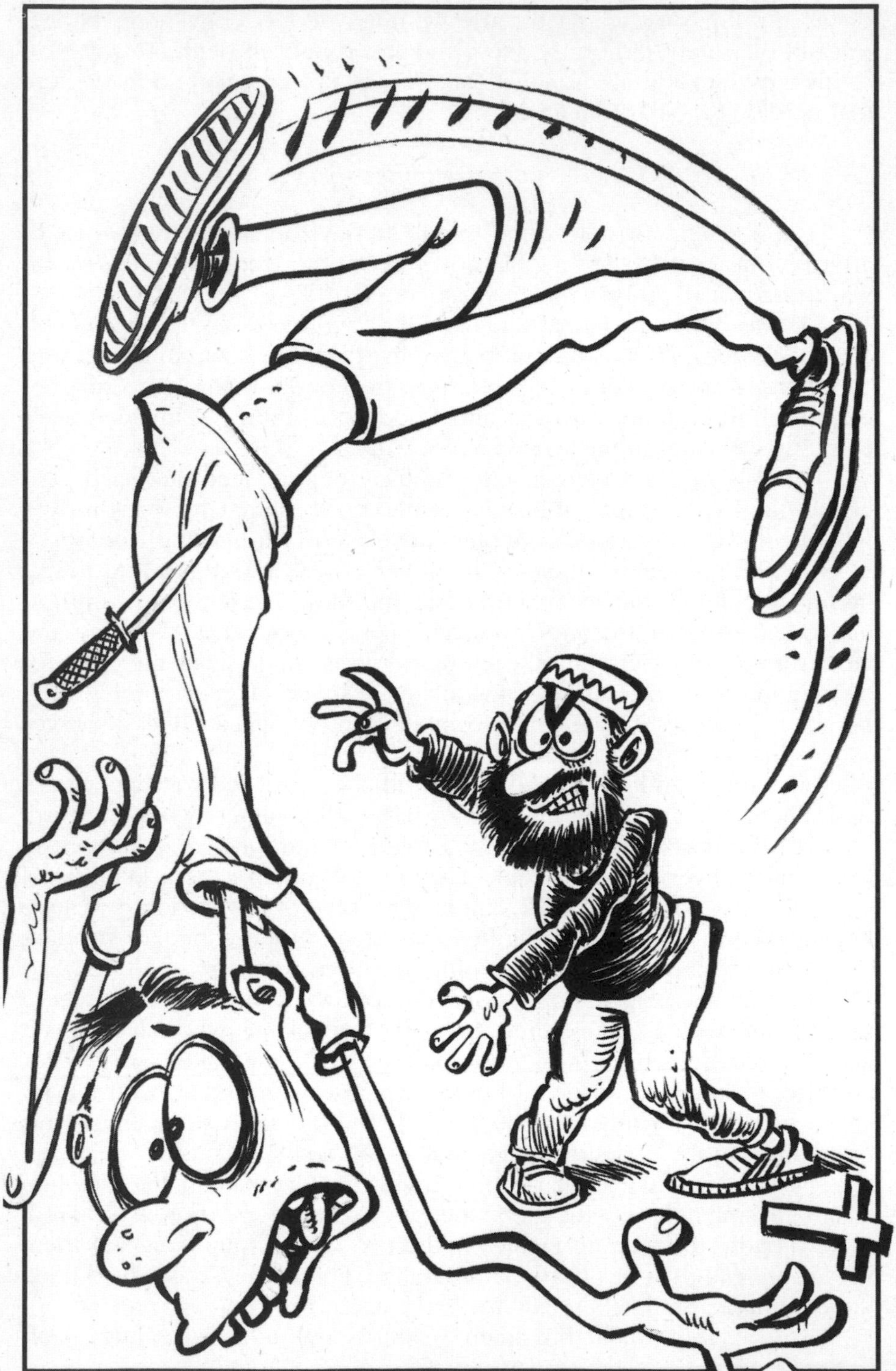

or he'd call the police. He backed away, still smiling, but didn't bother Al again. Al's seen him at shows since but the fan just says hello and doesn't follow him any more.

Though Al's worst encounter of the mad fan kind was at one of the London UKCACs when some kind of Christian Fundamentalist knob-head approached him and demanded that he should repent his sins, convert to Christianity and burn all copies of *The Spiral Cage*. The loony claimed that Al would go to hell for his unbridled blasphemy–that of claiming that he had cured himself of Spina Bifida symptoms when, as well he should know, only Great God Almighty had the power to do that.

Al tried to be polite but the guy continually harassed him. Quoting great chunks of the Bible, he followed Al around the whole weekend in a relentless attempt to harangue him into changing his wicked ways.

Eventually, when Al was about to leave, still quite unrepentant of his alleged sins, the outraged comic "fan" pulled a knife on him in the lobby of the con building.

Now, Al's not the sort of guy you should fuck around with. He's a black belt in karate and has practised Shaolin Kung Fu for around thirty years, not to mention a frightening catalogue of other martial arts. He's taken guns from muggers in the past. Before he could blink, the religious nut job was disarmed before having his head smashed into a drinks machine. Al then calmly pinned him down till the police arrived.

My own "Mad Fan" story isn't as extreme but was still a bit perturbing.

Travelling back from a talk at Exeter University during the *Luther Arkwright* UK tour in 1989, I thought myself lucky to get a table to myself in a crowded train. At Bristol Parkway station, a hirsute and unshaven guy wearing a stained tee-shirt and jeans burst into the carriage, waving around a half full beer glass and proclaiming proudly to the passengers that he's just ripped it off from the station bar.

Please bear in mind that throughout the following exchange he was shouting, not just talking to me but addressing the whole carriage, occasionally rising from his seat and waving his arms as if he was giving a speech.

Spotting the empty seat across the table, he stowed his duffle bag and sat down, all the while declaring "Fuck Maggie Thatcher! Fuck Maggie Thatcher! Bloody Fucking Maggie Thatcher!"

Not being overtly enamoured of the rabidly right-wing Prime Minister myself, I asked him what the matter was. He launched into a loud monologue liberally peppered with "fucking" before every noun, adjective and verb. Apparently, due to new government legislation, he was now forced to go to job interviews or his welfare money would be stopped.

He was travelling for a job interview in Manchester with the animation company *Cosgrove Hall*. Stuffed in his duffle bag was the presumably crumpled suit he was going to change into when he reached there. He was already two hours late for the interview but was convinced he would get the job because he'd once sold smack to a Dave Cosgrove! (Somebody, I imagine, with no connection whatsoever to Cosgrove Hall).

The other passengers were shifting uncomfortably in their seats, glancing nervously at the exit and avoiding his eyes as he swept his maniacal gaze around the carriage.

"That's right," he announced. "I used to be a fucking junkie–but not any more! Now I'm a fucking *COMICS JUNKIE!*"

Apparently he was also a comic artist, though not just a "fucking ordinary one": he did *graphic novels*–though he hadn't had any published yet. These seemed to consist of strips that he'd written and drawn for his wife while he was in prison. Still, he was now working on his magnum opus–a mind-numbingly original concept:

"See, it's like a fucking cross between *Superman* and *Flash Gordon*!"

I must have appeared dubious because he immediately launched into an evangelical tirade about how comics were a proper art form and how there were these really good comics nowadays. He crudely lectured me and the travelling public in general, listing all his favorites; *Watchmen*, *V For Vendetta*, *Spiderman*, *X-Men* and *2000AD* strips–especially *Nemesis the Warlock*, a strip I'd drawn for several years.

And he didn't even pay for his comic habit. Apparently, once a week he simply went into his local comic store, *Forever People*, with a couple of plastic bags and ripped off whatever he fancied. He was extremely proud of the fact and didn't seem to mind that he'd just informed the entire carriage.

Now, as I said, I was in the middle of a signing tour and was returning to Bristol the following week to sign at Forever People. The posters advertising the event hadn't gone unnoticed by this crackpot who was excitedly looking forward to it.

"Hey," he declared, "next fucking week Bryan Talbot's doing a fucking signing there!"

"Er…Bryan Talbot?" I ventured.

"Yeah, Bryan fucking Talbot!" he announced and proceeded to run through my entire publishing history, from *Brainstorm* through *2000AD* to *Arkwright* to the whole train. He was going to get them all signed by me next week!

Throughout all this I'd been determined to keep schtum about myself but, thinking of the scene in a week's time when he'd realize that I'd kept him in the dark, I said "Oh, thanks a lot. I'm glad you like the

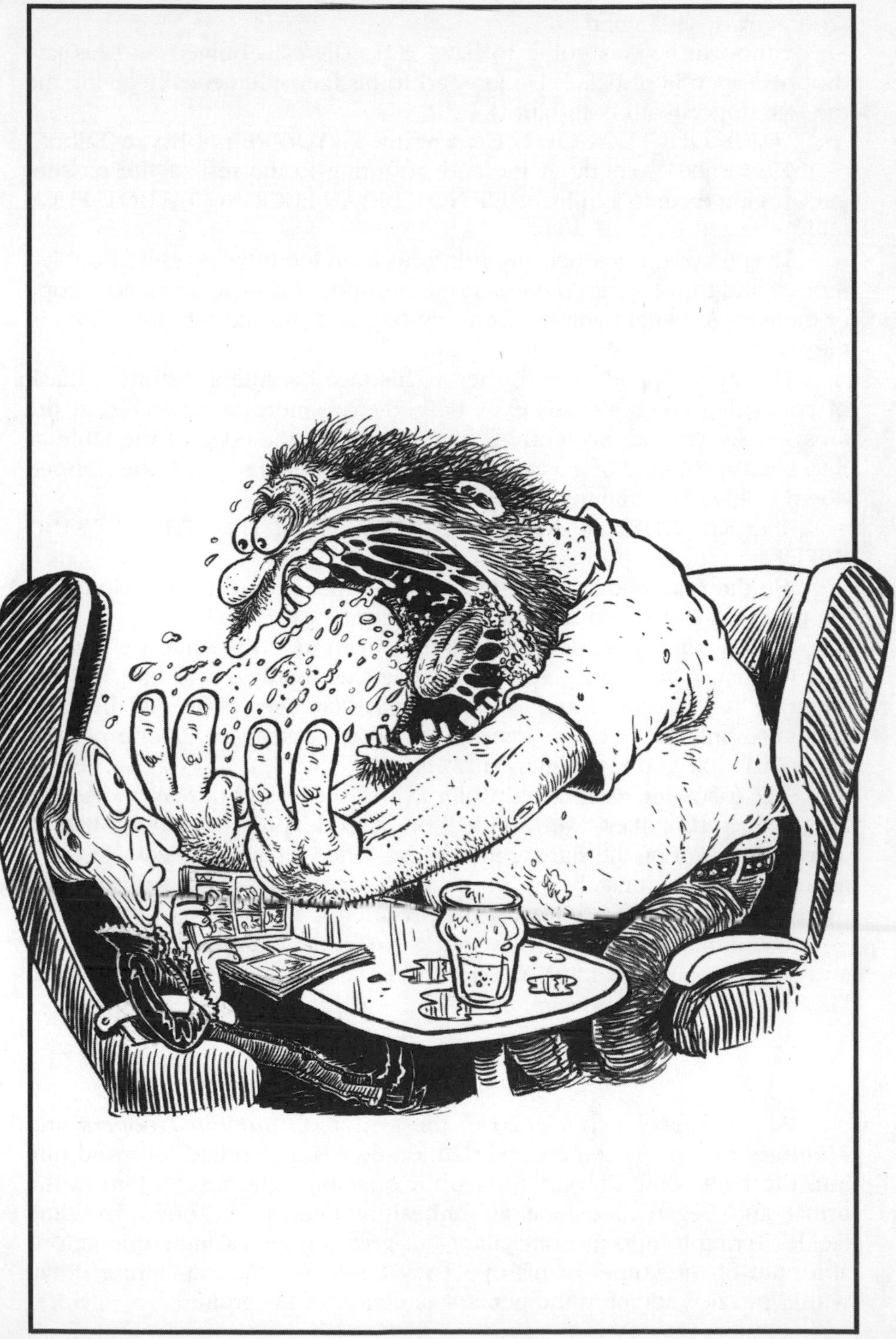

work. I'm Bryan Talbot".

I thought he was going to have a fit. His eyes bulged and his jaw dropped open in disbelief. He jumped to his feet, energetically giving me the two fingers with both hands.

"FUCK OFF! FUCK OFF!" He screamed. "*YOU'RE* not Bryan Talbot!"

He turned, pointing at me and gesturing to the rest of the passengers, urging them to join in. "HE'S NOT BRYAN FUCKING TALBOT! FUCK OFF!"

Desperately, I grabbed my portfolio from the luggage rack, fumbled it open and thrust some *Nemesis* originals under his nose. I pulled a copy of the new Arkwright volume from my bag and showed him my photo in the back.

His jaw dropped even further as his face became a distorting mask of conflicting emotions. His eyes bulged even more as he stared at the artwork, swaying on his feet, his hands gripping the edge of the table as if to keep some kind of grasp on reality. After several seconds, he flopped down in his seat, grinning widely.

"FUCKING HELL!" he shouted. "WAIT 'TILL I TELL THE FUCKING WIFE!"

He then ran off to the buffet, insisting that he had to be able to tell his pub mates that he'd bought Bryan Talbot a beer.

Shortly after he returned, the train pulled in at the station where he had to change for Manchester and he left as loudly as he had arrived, shouting his goodbyes and waving his stolen beer glass. As the train started to pull out from the station, the other passengers, as one person, turned to look at me and mimed "*Phew!*"

The following week I told Colin Evans, the owner of *Forever People,* about their shoplifter. We decided on a code phrase I could use to identify him during the signing and he stationed a couple of guys to keep an eye open. Fortunately my number one fan didn't show up. Even he must have realized that I'd warn the proprietor.

Did I mention that I'm working on a new graphic novel? It's a anus-clenchingly ground-breaking concept. See–it's like a cross between Flash Gordon and Superman.

––––––––––

At the Bristol Expo in 2006, the writer of *Starship Troopers* and *Midnight Kiss*, Tony Lee noticed that a rather large fan had followed him into the bathroom. The guy took up a position right next to him at the urinal and began to exhibit an unhealthy interest in Tony's wedding tackle. Trying to appear nonchalant but growing increasingly uncomfortable, out of the corner of his eye Tony could see the fan staring down with a puzzled squint in the general direction of his groin.

As they both turned around, zipping up, the fan declared "Ah, I sec! You're Tony Lee!"

Flabbergasted by this innovative and unusual means of identification, Tony stepped back, aghast. Was there, unbeknownst to himself, photographs of his todger being circulated widely within the fan community?

"What, you can recognize me from my knob?" he blurted.

"No, you silly sod," said the fan. "Your nametag!" and walked out, leaving Tony staring down at the con ID badge he'd carelessly pinned to the lap of his shirt.

One variety of fan that's guaranteed to strike terror in the heart of the comic pro is the type who approach you carrying unfeasibly large art portfolios—the amateur artist who somehow thinks that by running their work beneath your eyes you will either snap your fingers and conjure up a six-figure publishing deal or say a magic word that will make them draw better.

Having said that, over the years I've seen some sterling work this way by people who've often gone on to work in the industry but, I have to say, that's extremely rare. The standard is usually pretty mediocre and it's painfully embarrassing to have to stand there and desperately search for words that will convey something positive when asked to comment or advise. I never like telling people how they should draw anyway—everybody has their own style—so try and avoid it wherever possible.

At *Uncommoncon* in Dallas in late 2000, one guy proudly showed me a strip he'd written and drawn whose storytelling was so incomprehensible and whose artwork so astonishingly, mind-bogglingly awful that at first I was at an absolute loss as to what to say. He wanted advice but I didn't want to even start on the indescribably bad figure drawing, pacing, composition, lettering or inking, so I picked on something safe and technical, the perspective, which was a total unholy mess. If he'd been attempting a funny or surrealistic strip that required naïve or fucked-up perspective it would have been a different matter but here he was attempting a realistic adventure story.

"Er, I think that your perspective needs a little work," I ventured.

"Uh? Whaddaya mean?"

"Well, for example, see this scene here where this guy is in the doorway in the background?"

"Yeah?"

"Well, your placement of the eye level at his chest means that this table in the foreground must be about fifteen foot high. See—the horizon —your eye level—cuts through its legs. And, even if it's supposed to be that high, we'd actually be looking up at it from this angle, not down onto the top. And this cat here looks as if it's about three inches high and this window wouldn't be foreshortened like…"

He held up his hand, seemingly delighted.

"Fine. Show me how to do it."

I looked around. There were no other fans waiting to see me. My neighbour Rick Veitch had left his table to stretch his legs.

"Okay," I said. "Sit down."

I spent a good quarter hour quickly going through the rudimentary principles of perspective, filling sheet after sheet with sketchy explanatory diagrams. When we hit four-point perspective, I decided to spare him and returned instead to his comic panel, quickly redrawing it in rough on another sheet with a better placement of the eye level and introducing a vanishing point.

He stared at it for a while, smiling gleefully.

"Ah *knows* perspective now!" he exclaimed, "Ah couldn't see what the hell you was talkin' about before but now it's all clear! Ah *knows* perspective!"

He thanked me and walked off looking like someone who'd just experienced a Pauline conversion.

"Wait a minute," I called after him, "don't you want to take these sketches, y'know, for reference?"

"Don't need 'em!" He grinned, tapping his forehead. "Ah *knows* perspective now!"

And off he went. Take it from me, it takes longer than fifteen minutes to "know perspective".

———————

Grant Morrison and *Zenith* artist Steve Yeowell were signing in a Glasgow store when they were approached by an intense-looking geezer who wanted to show them his artwork. He'd allegedly come up with a mind-blowingly original scenario for a science fiction graphic novel and he wanted their opinion on the cast of cosmic characters he'd invented for it. They flipped through the plastic sheets of the portfolio containing headshot after headshot of almost identical fat grey monsters. No comic pages, scenes or full figures–just head shots. As their skimming grew faster, he suddenly stopped them by slamming a hand on a page. Pressing his face close to theirs, he pointed to one of the amorphous blobs and lowered his voice to a conspiratorial growl.

"This one…" he said, "…has *three* toes!"

———————

At a festival in Belo Horizonte in Brazil, I was drinking beer, sketching and chatting with fans round a large circular table when a guy pushed through the crowd in the bar and addressed me.

"Hey! Hey, Meester Talbot?"

"Yes?"

He pointed off into the crowd.

"Eez okay, my seester come, show you her draws?"

I nearly sprayed my beer out.

"Okay." I said and he ran off, leaving me literally crying tears of laughter and unable to explain to my Brazilian friends why, without cracking up again. After a while, he returned with his sister but I'm afraid I can't remember her drawings at all.

Later the same night, I found myself at a sidewalk restaurant drawing Batman on a young lady's thigh next to veteran Batman artist Jerry Robinson who was simultaneously drawing the Joker, a character he created, on her other thigh. It's a hard life being a comic artist.

Sometimes, you'll look through the portfolio of an up and coming artist and recognize an image–by which I mean it's a swipe. They've ripped off another artist. If I ask whether they made it up, they invariably claim they did. When this happens with someone you've previously met and respected, it's a real bummer. I really wish that I could quote Oscar Wilde on these occasions but I always chicken out. A wannabee poet once showed Wilde a vanity press edition of his works and asked him to write a comment on the title page.

"This work is both brilliant and original." wrote Wilde. "Unfortunately the brilliant bits aren't original and the original bits aren't brilliant."

No, no. Scrub that. One thing you don't want to be in these delicate situations is sarcastic. There's a good chance that the artist will either burst into tears or impale you with their 0.3 Rotring pen. And *never* try to be witty by quipping "Don't give up the day job!" They may reply "I already have." Either that or they'll turn out to be the next Frank Miller and after they're famous they'll endlessly rip the piss out of you by quoting it in interviews. Erstwhile *2000AD* art editor Robin Smith (now artist on *The Bogie Man*) once told Glenn Fabry, *Neverwhere* artist and one of the highest-paid cover illustrators in the business, that he'd never make a living in comics.

At the Bristol Expo a couple of years ago, a serious-looking dude, his portfolio clutched beneath his arm, arrived at Al Davison's booth and asked if he would take a look at his artwork. Al often does comic workshops and drawing lessons and said he would be happy to appraise the work. Opening the portfolio, Al was disconcerted to discover that the contents consisted entirely of large and excruciatingly dull watercolour paintings of tapeworms. Thinking that this was some sort of joke, Al looked up grinning at the fan who stared down expectantly, solemnly waiting for a comment. Swallowing a witticism, Al glanced back at the artwork, his attention drawn to the printed labels pasted to the bottom of each portfolio page. They read "Captain America", "The Thing", "The Hulk" and so on. The tapeworms, it transpired, had supposedly passed through the digestive tracts of different Marvel superheroes and been dug out of their respective turds. It wasn't a parody. He was seriously expecting the samples to get him work at Marvel. •

CHAPTER FOUR

THE DAMNED

Publishers of the most famous superhero comics in the world, Marvel and DC have many outstanding differences, historically, politically and stylistically, but the biggest and most striking difference becomes apparent as soon as you try to name a vibrator after one of their characters. With the conspicuous exception of *Superman*, most of DC's heroes' names would be absolutely naff if used as a buzz-cock brand name. They just wouldn't work. *Batman*? Rubbish. *Green Lantern*? Even if it was luminous, crap. *The Flash*? Over too quickly. *The Martian Manhunter*? Er, well, that's not *too* bad if it was aimed at the gay market. *Hawkman*? *Sandman*? *Aquaman*? Naff, naff, naff. *The Atom*? No way! *Deadman*? You gotta be joking. *Nobody* would buy electric phalluses with those names. Er, well, ahem, I wouldn't buy a vibrator anyway, obviously, that goes without saying–but that's not the point. Marvel, on the other hand, has a veritable cornucopia of possible vibrator-friendly comic book titles. Ladies and gentlemen, please cast your eyes in the general direction of… *Mister Fantastic*! *Iron Man*! *The Incredible Hulk*! *The Thing*! *The Mighty Thor*! *The Beast*! *Wolverine*! *Giant Man*! *The Punisher*! *Marvel Two-in-One*! *Marvel Triple Action*! *Iron Fist*! And let's not forget Dave Gibbons' favorite (for it was he who first alerted me to this phenomena): *Giant-Size Man-Thing*!

In actuality, for many British comic creators, the biggest difference between the two companies is that from the early eighties to the mid-nineties, when monthly comic sales were humungous and money no object, DC Comics actively headhunted Brit writers and artists, wining and dining us and, once a year, usually during the *UKCAC* weekend, throwing us a great big party.

I missed the first one, at London's legendary Savoy Hotel, but it has since become the stuff of legend itself. Presided over by then DC publisher Jenette Khan, the cream of British comic talent, completely nonplussed at being treated as valued freelancers for the first time in their lives and faced with as much free booze as they could pour down their collective gullets, did the only sensible thing and got well and truly plastered. Following the wine, the litres of expensive after-dinner brandy placed on the tables before them were quickly dispatched, some creators graduating to drinking straight from the bottle.

For poor Jenette and her editors, the anticipated sophisticated dinner party in the heart of five star luxury turned into an anarchic disaster area with creators passing out, crawling on the floor, throwing bits of haute cuisine at each other, singing disreputable songs, belching, farting and running to the toilet to puke. It was like a scene from a post-modern punk Marx Brothers movie directed by Ken Russell.

When *Judge Dredd* writer Alan Grant, *Slaine* writer Pat Mills and his wife Angie, three of the lucky few to emerge alive, finally staggered out into the street, they were obliged to step over the prostrate form of Alan's co-writer, big John Wagner, lying in the road outside the Savoy entrance.

"Get up, John," Alan said. "Come on, there's a taxi here."

"Leave me be," John slurred. "I'm going to sleep."

They left him to it, their cab having to navigate around his body.

But they weren't safe yet. Unfortunately, as the taxi set off, Alan swiftly and embarrassingly threw up all over Angie. Alan was so drunk that, when they reached the depths of the Essex countryside over an hour later, he couldn't direct the cab driver to his house so he was dropped off in a country lane and left to fend for himself.

Miles from home, he stumbled across fields, fell over walls, clawed through hedges and crawled down ditches before he finally arrived at his farmhouse at about four o'clock in the morning. He entered and, still too sozzled to turn a corner, walked straight into a stone wall and knocked himself out. No wonder that Alan is now a teetotaller.

Meanwhile, John Wagner had somehow managed to get to his feet and hailed a cab home. When he arrived, his girlfriend had gone to bed and he found that he was locked out, so he started throwing stones at her apartment windows. They didn't wake her, so John threw another, a little harder, this time shattering the glass. Waking up in her bedroom, his girlfriend thought a burglar was breaking in and immediately phoned the police. After being spread over the hood of a police car and grilled at some length, he was eventually allowed inside.

The following year the DC party was a much more sedate affair and took place in the swish *Serpentine* restaurant in Hyde Park, hired for the evening by DC. I wasn't invited myself. DC had never heard of me. I blagged my way along as Alan Moore's guest. This meant that my name wasn't even included on their guest list, which made my subsequent meeting with Jenette Khan a thing of wonder. She really does have a mind like a steel trap: she misses nothing. When Alan and I got there she was formally greeting people by he door as they arrived. She shook hands with Alan and exchanged some pleasantries, myself eclipsed by his large and hairy form.

As he moved on, he rumbled "This is my guest, Bryan Talbot."

"Pleased to meet you," she responded and Alan and I went to find a table the other side of the crowded restaurant, close by the string quartet. That was it. I was never close enough to talk with her for the rest of the night.

At one point, she thought it would be a good idea to hire a gipsy trio (in reality three cockneys in fancy dress) to circulate and serenade her guests. This is a definition of "good" that I hadn't previously encountered. She sent them over to the table where Alan and Sue Grant and John Wagner were sitting. Finding that they were unable to have a conversation with the accordion blasting into their ears, John beckoned one over after they finished a number.

"Yes, signor?" he said. "Do you have a request for us?"

"Yes, " said John. "Fuck off."

One year later, the party was held at the glitzy Soho restaurant and bar, *Bill Stickers*. This time I went along as the guest of *Robohunter* artist Ian Gibson, which meant that, again, I wasn't listed as attending: nobody knew I was going. Ian had phoned me the day before to tell me that he couldn't make it due to impending deadline doom, but I went along anyway.

Jenette was welcoming the guests in the entrance lobby and had her back to me as I walked in as she chatted to Trina Robbins and Steve Leialoha. As they headed off inside, she turned on her heel and was confronted by myself struggling to concoct a credible explanation for gate crashing. She didn't even bat an eye.

"Bryan!" she said. "So glad you could come!"

After that, I received an official invitation every year.

I spent that evening with Trina and Steve, never having met them before but having corresponded with Trina after I commissioned a strip from her for *Near Myths* several years earlier. Bill Stickers was crammed with all sorts of expensive memorabilia and we actually ate at Marilyn Monroe's marble dinning table.

During one San Diego Comicon, Jenette and Vertigo editor Karen Berger took Jamie Delano, Neil Gaiman and me to a posh eatery down on the bay. By this time I was actually working for DC, drawing the *Hellblazer Special* and *The Nazz* and we were to talk about me doing some *Sandman* pencils. We had to wait in the bar, as our table wasn't ready, so I fired up a cigarette, an admittedly disgusting and objectionable habit that I had at that time. I'd only just done so when the waiter reappeared to tell us we could now be seated and we followed him to a table set apart and surrounded on three sides by large windows, the top halves of which were open and looking out over the bay.

Millionaire Jenette was dressed, as ever, in the height of fashion, her hair exquisitely sculpted into a bouffant fantasy.

As I was pulling up a chair, the waiter tapped me on the shoulder and whispered discretely "Excuse me sir. This is a non-smoking restaurant. You can only smoke in the bar area."

"No bother," I said and cast around for an ashtray.

Of course, there were none on the table but there were the open windows behind Jenette. Taking a long last pull on the Marlboro, which made the end glow like a furnace, I flicked it firmly towards the window with startling accuracy. It described a perfect arc through the air, heading at great speed for the center of the open window through which the stars and the lights on the other side of the water twinkled prettily in the hot San Diego night. Upon reaching the window the cigarette spectacularly exploded, sending a shower of sparks and fire cascading over Jenette, who let rip with a shriek so piercing the eardrums of everyone within a radius of thirty feet were permanently damaged.

It appeared that the open windows were covered with a fine black mesh–a mosquito net–near invisible against the dark outside.

Neil and I rushed over and aided her in frantically brushing the burning ash from her hair and coat. I was mortified but Jenette immediately regained her composure and, apart from the lingering whiff of burnt hair and the occasional amusing discovery of a scorch mark on her Armani suit, the evening continued without incident. She didn't seem to take offense at my monstrous gaffe as I continued to work for DC for several years and still occasionally do so.

———————

The relationship between publishers and their creators is always, of course, an unequal one. Publishers can drop an artist on a whim, unless they are the flavor of the month and have a gold-plated exclusivity contract. These only last a year or two anyway and are no guarantee of future employment. For this reason, it's a vital necessity that you don't piss off your publishers or their minions, the editors, who hold your very financial stability in their promiscuous hands. Missing a deadline is a time-honored way to speedily achieve this and there are many stories told in the pro bar of the extreme lengths that comic artists and writers will go to in order to finish the work on time.

I once worked fifty-six hours straight, had one hour's sleep, got up, had a shower and got on the train to London to deliver the artwork. Half-asleep, I'd left Euston station and was battling with the London traffic before I realized that I'd left the artwork on the luggage rack. Luckily it and the train were still there, Euston being the train's terminus. I don't do that sort of stuff these days, thank Kirby, now that I work on graphic novels in my own sweet time.

Working on a monthly or weekly title, it's inevitable that at some point, stupid or utterly nasty events will conspire to keep time from being on your side. This is an unholy consequence of *Parkinson's First Law*, which states that any work will expand to fill the time available, colliding with *Sod's Law*, which is a real bugger: anything that can go wrong will go wrong.

During the nineties, when Image comics could afford to throw money around like it was going out of fashion, creators could get away with all kinds of procrastination. Many writers worked Marvel-style, writing the script only after the artists had illustrated their plot. Before the days of digital files, this caused many problems if an artist was late, often resulting in someone having to take a last-minute flight to deliver the completed lettering to the printer in order to meet the shipping date. I believe that this caused the nervous breakdown of at least one Image editor.

The most extreme example I know of an artist meeting a deadline in the face of adversity, come what may, is that of Al Davison. In the late nineties he was drawing *Vermillion*, written by Lucius Shepard, for DC's SF imprint *Helix* when he contracted the extremely debilitating disease *Myalgic Encephalomyelitis*, otherwise known as M.E. or Chronic Fatigue Syndrome.

He'd penciled and inked the first two issues before he developed Carpal Tunnel Syndrome as a side effect of the M.E. This affects the nerves in the hands, making it very painful to use them. So the editor decided that Al needed an inker.

"No way!" said Al, knowing that having to produce tight pencils for someone else to ink would be every bit as hard as producing loose pencils and inking them himself. Plus he'd be lose the inker's fee, but he was overruled and an inker was brought in. Drawing very tight pencils made his hand increasingly worse until it completely seized up and induced an M.E. attack, making his muscles painfully weak, his vision impaired and leaving him unable to sit upright.

To meet the deadlines, Al penciled three whole issues with his left hand, lying on his back on the lower mattress of a bunk bed, with a drawing board strapped to the underside of the top bunk and with only one eye working.

Douglas Addams, renowned author of *The Hitch-hiker's Guide to the Galaxy*, once said "I like deadlines. I love the sound they make as they *whoosh* by".

Late for a deadline, artist Neal Adams, probably best known for his sterling work on *Batman* and *Green Lantern/Green Arrow,* allegedly claimed that he'd been mugged on the subway and had his portfolio containing the artwork stolen. It's said that he subsequently used this as an excuse over the next few months every time he was late on a job until he was finally caught out. This happened when the artwork involved was actually commissioned after the supposed robbery.

The same excuse was used in the eighties by an artist who shall remain nameless, when Lee Nordling was packaging the range of *He-Man* comics that accompanied the Mattel toys. First the guy said he was late because his girlfriend had had a miscarriage. Lee was very sympathetic and cut him some slack. Then, when his new deadline was up and he was supposed to bring the pages into Lee's office, he claimed that he'd been mugged in a parking lot and the felon had run off with his portfolio containing the finished job.

Lee gave him more time to redo the pages. The third deadline arrived and the artwork didn't so he phoned the firm the artist worked for to enquire where the hell the pages were. He wasn't there so Lee left an angry message with the person who'd answered the phone, who turned out to be the artist's boss. The guy blew his top and, after much wrangling, had a phone conference with the artist, lawyers for both sides and the art director at Mattel.

It now became apparent that the artist had only completed a grand total of two and a half pages. He denied ever being mugged and insisted that Lee had fabricated the whole thing. Fortunately the art director believed Lee, who never spoke to the artist, once his friend, again. The guy went on to become a highly-paid art director at a major amusement park.

Dez Skinn tells of a time when he was working for IPC children's comics in the early seventies. The usually infallible and highly prolific Leo Baxendale, the creator of the *Bash Street Kids* and many other classic Brit kid's comic characters, was up against the deadline. Instead of the artwork, he mailed a pair of trousers to his editor. When the guy phoned him to ask what the hell he was doing sending him his pants, Leo replied "Oh my God! I must have posted the artwork to the dry cleaners!"

This apocryphal story was actually doing the rounds for years before, attributed to various artists.

In a desperate moment, **Batman** and **Of Bitter Souls** artist Norm Breyfogle once spontaneously created an imaginary ectopic pregnancy for his girlfriend as an excuse for being late.

The offices of 2000AD used to have an "excuse-o-meter" on which the editorial team used to record artists reasons for blowing a deadline. One creator, believed to be **Judge Dredd** artist John Cooper, was forgiven a missing deadline because, tragically, his mother-in-law had died and he had to arrange the funeral. On   consulting the excuse-o-meter, it was discovered that he'd already used the same excuse the previous year.

Golden Age comic artist Irv Novick, who drew superhero strips for DC until the late nineties, is said to have used the "death in the family" excuse to the point where his mother had allegedly died several times.

Artist George Roussos, aka George Bell, also began his long career in the Golden Age of comics but is perhaps best known for his inking of Jack Kirby Silver Age classics such as **The Avengers**. According to this story he developed such a reputation for being late that many editors wouldn't use him. In the 1970s two editors working for Marvel had a meeting. They needed an artist to pencil a fill-in issue and they needed one soon.

"Hey," said one. "What about George Roussos? He's pretty good."

"Nah," said the cynical other. "Too slow."

"I'm gonna give him a try."

"You'll be sorry."

Undeterred, he gives George the job. After a month, the cynic enters the other's office.

"How's George doing on that strip?"

To stick to the schedule he needed to have finished at least half of the twenty-four page book by this point .The editor phones him up.

"Hi George. How's it going?"

"Fine," says George. "I'm just drawing page sixteen."

The editor grins triumphantly at the cynic, who's astounded.

"That's great," says the editor. "Can you send the first fifteen pages in so we can get them lettered?"

"Oh," says George, "I haven't done those yet."

This story is quite suspect. For one thing, neither the comic title nor the editors are named. For another, George was almost exclusively inking around this time. It is **told** though, which is the only criteria it needs to get in this book. Perhaps it happened to another artist and the name was changed in the retelling, as is the nature of these things.

———————

Mike Sekowsky, most famous for drawing *Justice League of America* and *Wonder Woman* in the sixties, was an extremely fast artist who never missed a deadline. He could pencil a monthly comic story in a week. Hearing of this, his editor, allegedly Julie Schwartz, called him into his office and started criticising his artwork, accusing Mike of hacking it out and telling him to take more time over the work in future.

Mike, not usually known for taking shit, surprisingly agreed. A month later he brought in the artwork for the next issue and showed it to the editor.

"Ah, that's it!" said Julie. "This is far superior!"

He proceeded to go through the whole strip, panel by panel, pointing out specific examples of how the artwork was so much better now that Mike was taking his time over it. When he'd finished, Mike calmly told him that he'd pencilled the strip in a week, as usual, and just kept it at home for three more weeks. The matter was never raised again.

As an aside, when *JLA* was first published in 1960, famous Marvel editor and writer Stan Lee, on hearing the impressive sales figures of the book, determined that Marvel should publish its own superhero team title. Rather than slavishly copy the JLA format, with artist Jack Kirby, he created the *Fantastic Four*, kick-starting the Marvel renaissance.

———————

Speaking of old stories, this one's so venerable that people stand as a mark of respect when it's told. It's nothing to do with deadlines but it's still in the area of editor/artist relationships.

Thought of by many as one of the greatest comic artists ever, though always outspoken and somewhat volatile, Alex Toth went into the DC offices in the late forties to collect a check from his editor, Julie Schwartz. This is in the days before they began to mail them out to the contributors. Toth's job had been accepted and he was told that his payment was just waiting to be collected. He arrives at Julie's room to find that he's out of the office for the day, so he asks the editor who's sharing the room, the equally outspoken and often offensive Robert Kanigher, to find his check.

Kanigher, who worked in comics for over five decades, writing and editing many classic DC characters, rummages in Julie's desk drawer and pulls out the check. He turns to Toth.

"You know," he smirks, "I think your work stinks." And tears up the check right in front of him.

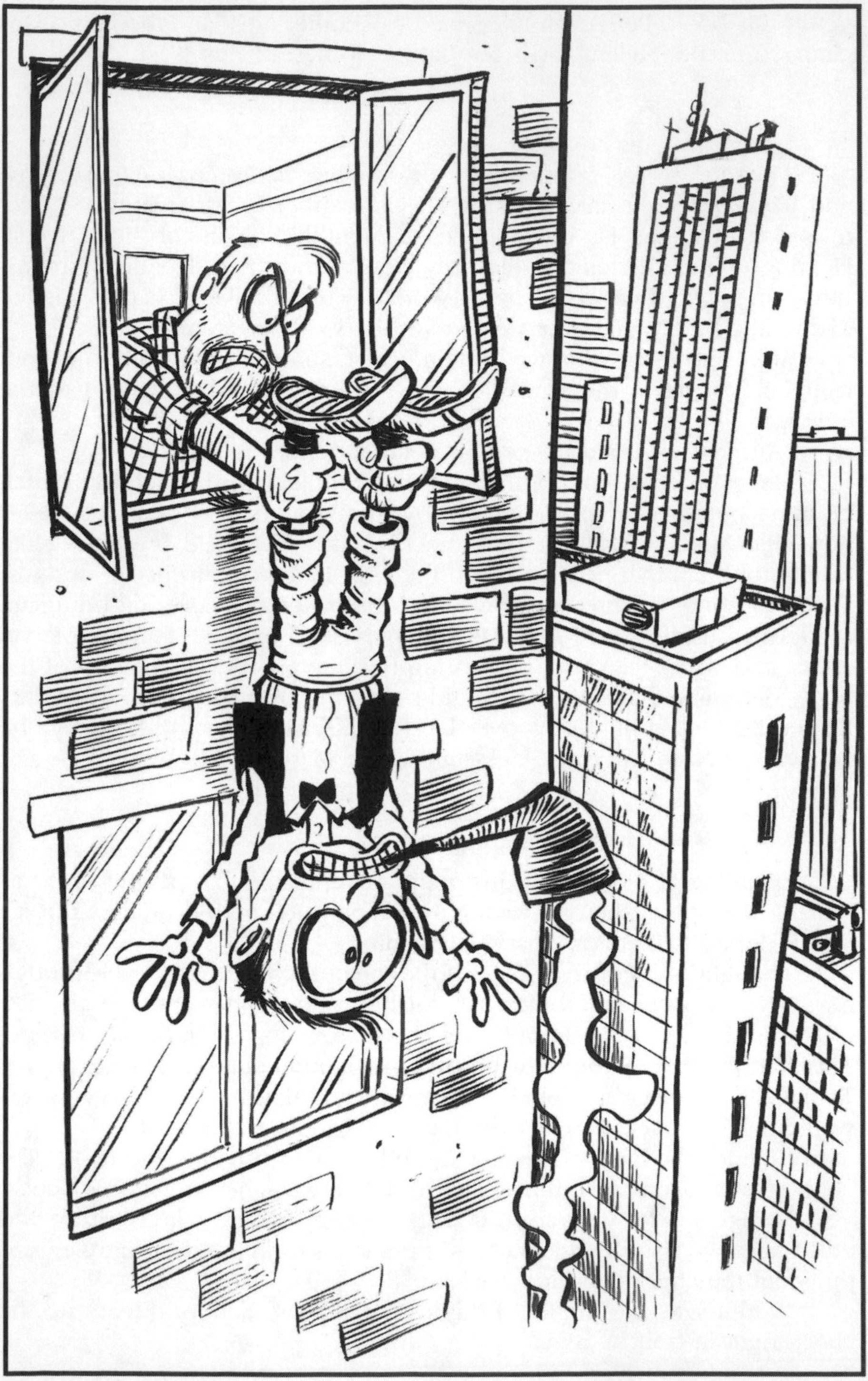

The first the DC office staff that day know of this is when they hear blood-curdling screams issuing from Julie's office. They burst in to find Alex Toth dangling Kanigher out of the office window by his ankles.

The above is sometimes told with the role of the creator played by Ed Herron, Jim Mooney or Harlan Ellison. However, it's always Robert Kanigher who's the one being dangled.

In the 1950s he once burst into a meeting of creators attempting to form a Comics Artists' Union.

"None of you are artists!" he declared. "You're nothing but a bunch of useless, replaceable hacks and you should be grateful to us for giving you any work in the first place!"

It's true to say that Mort Wiesinger, most famous as the editor of DC's *Superman* line in the sixties, was not particularly well-liked. At his funeral many creators reportedly turned up just to make sure he was dead. As the service drew to a close, people were standing around the grave in silence.

"Would anyone like to say a few words about the dear departed?" they were asked.

One of the funeral party stepped forward and cleared his throat.

"Well," he said, "his brother was worse." •

CHAPTER FIVE

SELLING COMICS FOR FUN AND PROFIT

O kay, already–these aren't stories. They're not even funny. But if you've never heard of these places, you really should.

We all have an image of the stereotypical comic store, from a mixture of personal experience and *The Simpsons*; the famous boys' locker room scenario where a geek sales clerk holds court to a handful of geek fanboys, displaying his superior knowledge gleaned from being "in the business" and glares disdainfully at any member of the public who's had the misfortune to wander in accidentally or out of sheer curiosity. Comics spill from cardboard boxes piled in the middle of the unswept floor. The windows are decorated with embarrassing plastic toys, homoerotic posters of muscle-bound thugs wearing tights and pinups of half-naked bimbos with melon-sized breasts and sharp, spiky weapons. We've all been in one.

Fortunately, the majority are better than this caricature but, even so, they still share with it much of what makes comic stores merely outlets for a tiny niche market. Most offer to the bemused passer-by a bewildering barrage of bizarrely-dressed dolls and esoteric magazines (amazing as this seems, to normal people comics *are* esoteric). This makes them a little like martial arts weapons stores or stamp collectors' emporiums–you just wouldn't venture in there unless you were part of the tiny and mentally suspect minority to whom the stores deal.

Although the graphic novel market is building, with GN sections now in most regular bookstores and libraries, many comic shops are struggling to keep their heads above water. But there's one in Nottingham, now in its tenth year, whose profits increase annually, well above their sales projections. It's called *Page 45*. This is in a town with three other large comic stores nearby.

You want to open a comics store? You want to make some money? Follow Page 45's example. As co-founder Stephen Holland says "It's not rocket science". Their philosophy is very, very simple; why try and sell comics to a statistically tiny percentage of the   population when you can try and sell them to *everybody*? That's right, Page 45 is a comic store that appears to be a regular mainstream bookshop that any uninitiated civilian would feel comfortable about entering.

For a start, the store is right up there on the high street, not tucked away in a basement down a back alley beneath a gaudy sign reading *Lobo's Lair*. You can't afford the high street? Get a loan.

Their name, simply lettered, white on black, is non-committal, non-genre–not something that the owners think is way cool but sounds moronic to the general public. As opposed to the usual garish displays of toys and adolescent male power fantasies, Page 45's windows are black showcases, elegant and tasteful, each usually displaying a single graphic novel and blow-ups of a couple of its panels. The displays are changed monthly.

The doors are always open wide, even in winter, so it's easy for passing trade to stroll into from the street and browse. And they do. Accessible non-genre comic albums that would immediately interest the general public are the first thing you see when you enter; stuff to entice non-comic readers. Inside, the shelves are   classic black oak with GNs displayed cover-out, not the usual box racks. There's nice music playing at a reasonable volume. No posters or stickers or life-sized cutouts of Wolverine, just a couple of framed prints.

The staff is well motivated and mingles with the customers, chatting to them and recommending books. It's part of their job.

Page 45 specializes in graphic novels, something with a much higher profit margin than monthly comics. They always keep full runs of books in stock–every single *Cerebus* album, *Sandman, Bone* etc. When they sell out of an album, they re-order. What an alien concept! Rather than thinking "Wow! We sold all the copies of that graphic novel! Phew!" they think "Wow! That book sells! Let's get more copies!"

They carry all the quality small press books. As unbelievable as this sounds to most comic retailers, these are far more likely to sell to Joe Q Public than superhero comics, which, unsurprisingly, only sell to super-hero fans.

And–and this is the clever bit–they *do* carry superhero and manga titles but these are all tucked away in their own section right at the back of the store. Just think about it for a second–the comic fans who buy these titles are going to come in and buy them *ANYWAY!* There's no need to draw these customers in. Superhero fans are there, come hell and highwater. Instead Page 45 concentrates on selling books to 99.9% of the population.

And it works. I've seen a blue-rinsed eighty-year old lady in a tweed suit wander in demanding "And what sort of a shop is this, then?" and walk out five minutes later clutching a GN. The place is always full of customers and there are actually women on their own (in a comic shop?). In fact, there's a whole popular section devoted to women's comics.

Sadly and shockingly, co-founder Mark Simpson, dubbed "the John Peel of comics", died suddenly last year of a rare medical syndrome. His business partner Stephen Holland remains evangelical about comics and committed to maintaining the excellence of the store. The industry needs retailers with the vision of these guys. If any of you know someone who's thinking of starting a comic store, please tell 'em about Page 45.

———————

Of course, Page 45 is following the example of stores in France where comics are generally accepted as an art form and the general public no longer needs to be educated into reading them. There's no distinction made there between ordinary folk and comic fans.

Established in 1987, *The Beguiling* in Toronto is said to be the best comic store in North America and, from what I hear, shares much of Page 45's philosophy. Another successful store specializing in graphic novels, one directly inspired by a visit to Page 45 by US retailer Greg Bennett, is *Big Planet Comics* in Bethesda, Washington DC.

———————

I briefly mentioned the *Cosmic Comic Café* in chapter one. This is a large bar in Turku, the second biggest city in Finland after Helsinki. The CCC was started in the late nineties by a dozen comic fans who chipped in money to get it started after one of them woke up one morning and asked himself "What are the most important things in life?" His conclusion is writ large across the CCC's plate glass windows: "Beer and Comics".

Beginning with one unit in a city centre shopping mall, they expanded to four, buying up properties on either side as they became vacant and knocking the walls through.

The bar hosts monthly exhibitions of comic art displayed all around the walls. There's an extensive library of comics and comic albums which customers can read whilst in the bar and a large selection of games from chess to *Monopoly* and *Trivial Pursuit* through to role-playing fantasy games. It's quite amazing to be in this crowded bar at two in the morning and see, among the clientele simply socializing, people sitting on their own engrossed in graphic novels. For quite a few years they also sold comics: the original idea was for it to be a bar/shop but they had to wind that side down as the place is that popular a venue that they need all the space they can get.

As a way of encouraging the public to read comics it really works there in Finland. And that's the sad part for me. Finns seem to be able to be polite and well behaved, even after drinking all night. In Britain a place like this would never work. It would quickly be spoilt by drunken yobs. The comics and games would be defaced, torn up or stolen. Would it work in the USA? •

CHAPTER SIX

THE GOOD, THE BAD, THE FREQUENTLY INEBRIATED

As you've no doubt gathered by now, certain comic writers and artists are the raw material of legend. They can't help but generate stories. Others are as dull as ditchwater but I'm not going to talk about them. Who can forget the time a famous writer, during his *Eagle Award* acceptance speech, said "Either be hot or cold or the Lord shall spew you forth"? Well, me for a start.

Here are some of the stories worth the telling. Most of these have never been repeated outside the hallowed walls of convention pro bars, but I'll begin with one that *was* highly publicized.

———————

The celebrated feud between Dave Sim and Jeff Smith began one night when Dave was visiting Jeff and his wife Vijaya Iyer. Dave had been the leading light of the US comic self-publishing movement for many years until eclipsed by Jeff's success. I've always wondered whether this was the reason behind the subsequent debacle. He'd also been concocting a bizarre misogynistic belief system along the lines of *Men are From Mars and Women are From Hell* and become insanely terrified of the concept of feminism, believing that only himself and a handful of other "free thinkers" are the only ones on the planet not to have been brainwashed in a sort of feminist *Invasion of the Body Snatchers* scenario. The fact that patriarchy has already successfully done this for thousands of years doesn't seem to have occurred to him.

In the eighties I once spent an hour or two smoking grass in a hotel room with Dave and, believe me, once he has it in his head to talk about something, he'll do it and there's no way to get him to change the subject. He talked about all this cool stuff he'd put into *Cerebus the Aardvark* without me being able to get in a single word to tell him that I'd never ever read the bloody thing. I saw the first issue when it came out, flipped through it and put it back on the rack, dismissing it as the Barry Smith *Conan* parody that it was. How did I know that it would become a book that would be so experimental and energetic in pushing the boundaries of the comic medium? I did pick up the "telephone book" collections much later, when Dave visited while on his UK tour in the nineties.

Anyhow, at Jeff and Vijaya's dinner table he starts in on his whole "women are bloodsuckers" shtick to the point of embarrassing, head-banging tedium. Documenting the occasion shortly afterwards in *Cerebus*, Dave paints an image of Vijaya that night as a malevolent Yoko Ono-like succubus figure feeding on Jeff's creative energy and goes on to say that the debate concluded after Jeff begged him to not reveal the secret nature of women to him in front of his wife. What's wrong with this picture?

Vijaya, as Jeff's *Cartoon Books* partner is one of the reasons for his incredible success. Acting as his agent and business manager, she does all the hard legal and organisational stuff while Jeff has fun all day writing and drawing.

The first time Jeff mentioned the "incident" was in an interview quite a few years later when he disclosed that it had actually concluded when he told Dave that, if he didn't shut the fuck up, he'd take him outside and deck him.

After stewing in his own juices for a year, Dave responded by publishing an open letter to Jeff demanding that they settle this thing man-to-man, with a boxing match. Dark Horse editor, Diane Schutz, resigned as Dave's long-time proofreader in disgust. Jeff simply told him to "get stuffed".

Okay. You're up to speed. So, some while later, after the scrap has been keenly anticipated at any convenient con by fanboys up and down America, Jeff accepts an invite to a European convention on the same weekend as the Mid-Ohio con, a local one for Jeff, who usually attends. After it's announced that he won't be there, Dave announces that he will be.

A few weeks before the event, Jeff's Euro invite falls through and he's left in somewhat of a dilemma. Does he avoid his local con and hide at home or should he go and inevitably bump into Dave, perhaps creating the situation where the challenge of a fist fight must go ahead?

He decides upon the latter course of action. Now Jeff is pretty well-built anyway, using the gym several times a week, but he decides to really prepare for this, just in case he needs to defend himself. He does an intensive course with the gym's resident martial arts black belt over the next couple of weeks to a stage where he's pretty hot.

On the first day of the con, he psyches himself up and goes on in there. Dave is sitting at a table signing, surrounded by fans.

Jeff walks straight up to it, leans over as says "Hi Dave? How's it going?"

Dave's absolutely flabbergasted at seeing him there.

"Oh, er, fine. And you?"

Dave's sweating. He's older than Jeff, a bit overweight and noticeably out of condition. No contest.

"Fine. See you later then," Jeff says and walks off.

There's been no talk of a boxing match since. The following year, Dave and Jeff "teamed up" in an art auction to raise money for the victims of the 2004 tsunami.

Now Igor Goldkind was a guy who provoked extreme reactions. People seemed to love him or loathe him. He entered the British comic scene when he took on the job of PR for Titan Books in the 1980s and was instrumental in establishing Will Eisner's preferred term "graphic novel" during the first GN boom when he either created the UK media hype around *Watchmen* and *The Dark Knight Returns* or was lucky enough to be in the right place at the right time, depending on your bias. He later worked as PR for IPC and even wrote for *2000AD* for a while, notably *The Clown* and *Judge Hershey* until he quit comics forever after a drunken argument with Alan Grant.

I suspect that this was during a particularly drunken weekend during a Glasgow Comic Art Convention when he was so alarmingly razzled he alienated a whole bunch of people, though perhaps I'm blending a couple of GLASCACs together here.

One night, the IPC expense account card jingling in his pocket, he returns to the *Copthorne Hotel* in the center of Glasgow with a large party of liggers he's just taken for dinner. Unfortunately for him, it's after eleven o'clock and Igor, not being a resident, is refused entry by the doorman. The bar in the Copthorne used to stay open until four or five in the morning or whenever the British comic community drank it dry. This is the happening place–and Igor's denied access.

He goes ballistic. He swears at the doorman, who, unimpressed, tells him to bugger off. Looking inside, through the plate glass door, Igor happens to spot Will Simpson, artist of *Rogue Trooper* and *Vamps*, crossing the lobby with a pint in his hand.

"You can't keep me out!" screams Igor. "See that guy? He works for me!"

"No I don't," shouts back Will. "I work for *2000AD*!"

The doorman tells Igor that if he doesn't piss off he'll call the police and shuts the door, locking him and his cronies out.

Infuriated, Igor shouts "I don't care! Call the fucking police!" and starts kicking the glass door. That very instant a police siren sounds in the distance. Thinking it was coming for them, the entire gang flees into the Glagow night.

The next day a contrite and woefully hung-over Igor turns up at the con, to be met by con organiser Frank Plowright.

"Hey," says Frank, "the police were here looking for you! Did you break the glass on the hotel door last night and intimidate the doorman?"

Frank tells him that he's assured the cops that Igor will dutifully report to Queen Street police station.

Igor blanches. "Oh my God!" he says and quickly exits.

Frank's killing himself laughing. He was only pulling Igor's leg, the date being, in fact, April Fool's Day. The Copthorne hotel was next door to Glasgow's Queen Street railway station and Frank had picked the name at random, intending that Igor would wander about a bit, fail to find a police station and return to the con. Unfortunately, as it turned out, the police *DID* actually have an office in the station and Igor arrives there and turns himself in. After an embarrassing scene of confusion straight out of a bad sitcom, the Scottish police, like the doorman, tell him to bugger off and stop wasting their time.

In the souvenir booklet of the following UKCAC in 1990, an Alan Davis illustration showed Igor, his head stuck in the Copthorne's sliding glass doors, shouting "Let me in! Don't you know who I am? I'm important! Famous! Will Simpson works for me!"

———————

At one GLASCAC, it's said that Igor entered the hotel bar just as the long-legged and miniskirted wife of Norm Breyfogle was bending over to rummage through her bag on the floor. Out of impulse, his inhibitions annihilated by drink, he slapped her right across the ass. She slowly straightened up and turned to face him before planting a classic uppercut on his jaw, sending him flying backwards and over a table to land in a crumpled heap on the floor.

Anther version of this story has *Accident Man* writer Tony Skinner in the role of the bottom-slapper. The notoriously lecherous Skinner once appeared at a London con with a giggling teenage bimbo hanging on each arm. He repeatedly introduced them with the line "This is Quim and this is Pussy."

Now, this ass-slapping and uppercut story is very well-established in UK pro bar history. I've heard it many times and it's always Norm Breyfogle's wife who's the slappee so, while giving this text a final read-through before sending it Moonstone, I decided to ask him about it.

I was surprised to hear that Norm has absolutely no knowledge of any such incident. He's never heard of either Igor Goldkind or Tony Skinner. More to the point, he's never been married and he's never been to Glasgow, though he did once attend a UK con, in London. This story is right up there in the realm of pure myth.

———————

The first Glasgow cons were organised by genial John McShane, at that time one of the proprietors of the Glasgow comic bookstore AKA, alongside Bob Napier and the wilfully lugubrious Pete Root. The first one-day con was themed around *2000AD* and a bunch of London-based artists arrive the night before. John meets them and takes them out to visit some especially good pubs. Several of the creators, a little anxious on their first trip to Glasgow at a time when the city had a very bad reputation for its gangs and hard men, express their apprehension about walking around the city center at night.

"Och, no," says John, "it's fine. I'll take you to some really nice pubs."

They arrive at the first pub. It's a burnt-out shell. John's shocked. He was drinking there the previous night.

"Never mind," he says. "There's another close by. "

Arriving in the bar, the first guy they see is bleeding all down one side of his face. They decamp to a third pub.

"This is much safer." John assures them.

It seems okay until a drunken regular holds a bread knife to Kevin O'Neill's throat for some reason best known to himself. Kevin, currently the artist of *The League of Extraordinary Gentleman*, laughs at this bit of tomfoolery and the guy, seemingly satisfied, wanders off.

———————

Bob Napier once invited Dave Gibbons to AKA to do a signing.

"I don't like your work," said Bob in all honesty, "but I'm a completist."

To his eternal credit, Dave sportingly accepted and had a huge turnout.

The first time Dave was in Glasgow, John McShane met him at Central Station. Dave was also concerned about the fearsome reputation of the city. Just as John was starting to tell him not to worry, Dave was accosted by a passing tough.

"Gee'us a fuckin' loan o' fifty pee, pal!"

"And how are you intending to repay this proposed loan?" Dave immediately replied.

The thug was so taken aback that John managed to drag Dave away before he was physically assaulted.

———————

Will Eisner, in Glasgow for the *Spirit Con* in 1985, bought a new cashmere coat while in the city. Hanging about in the lobby of the hotel before he and his wife Ann left, he still had his well-worn but treasured old coat draped over his arm, reluctant to part with it. Ann insisted that he did, so he gave it to Bob Napier, who took great pride in swanning around Glasgow wearing Will Eisner's coat for the next few years.

———————

One late night at GLASCAC, Marvel and DC superhero writer and artist Alan Davis walked into the gents of the Copthorne and discovered John McShane passed out and doubled over the toilet seat, with his pants round his ankles. With the help of *Comics International*'s Mike Conroy, he dressed John and carried him up to his hotel room. John comes to in the morning and finds, pinned up on his dressing table, a sketch by Alan of him unconscious in the toilet with his bare bum sticking in the air. The incident made such an impression on Alan that he redrew the scene for the illustration he contributed to the following UKCAC souvenir book in 1991.

———————

Anyhow, back to *enfant terrible* Igor Goldkind. One night during the tour to promote the weekly comic magazine *Crisis*, one of the attempts by IPC to reach a mature audience during the first GN boom, Igor and some of the writers and artists were in the bar of a Soho restaurant. Suddenly there was a commotion in the street outside and Igor decides to check it out.

Opening the door, he finds he's behind two big blonde guys in the middle of an impromptu photoshoot, surrounded by fans and uniformed minders. It was the then-famous boy band *Bros*. Igor didn't recognize them but nevertheless, perhaps thinking that here was a chance of some free publicity, tapped them on the shoulder.

"Hey, guys? Want to meet the artist who invented *Judge Dredd?*"

It turned out they were into *2000AD* and immediately left their fans to follow Igor to the bar area, where he introduced them to Carlos Ezquerra, the first Dredd artist, over from Spain especially for the tour. Igor left them to it and walked back to the others, who asked him who it was.

"No idea." he replied. "Some fucking pop star wankers."

It was one of those moments when the whole bar goes quiet for a moment and, in that moment, Igor's voice carried loud and clear over to the blonde twins who, for some reason, took offence. Igor was a recent immigrant to Britain from the USA and didn't even know what a wanker was at the time. The outraged Bros totally freaked out and started throwing things at him and threatening to break every bone in his body. He was saved by the prompt action of the group's own minders who forcibly removed them from the bar, with the help of half a dozen restaurant staff.

Shaking, Igor walked over to look out of the window to make sure they'd gone, only to be shocked by the ghastly white visage of one of the berserk Bros, his bared teeth and manic eyes making his face skull-like, looming through the darkness towards him. At the last minute, his minders grabbed hold of him and dragged him away down the street while he shook his fists and hurled abuse at Igor.

I heard the story the following week when the *Crisis* team of Carlos, John Wagner, Pat Mills, Jim Baikie and John Smith were on the Lancashire leg of the tour and stopped in Preston for an evening gig at the local Speculative Fiction Group. Igor insisted that they ate a full three course meal in the hotel restaurant where the speed of service was glacial, rather than the regular Indian place we usually used for guest speakers, resulting in them keeping the audience waiting for a good two hours.

Igor's crowning achievement, though, came during an Angoulême festival in the 1990s. At the time he was in some kind of partnership with Dez Skinn to produce manga editions in the UK and they'd been cultivating a relationship with a big Japanese publisher who had come over to the festival to meet up and discuss the project. Igor had hired a farmhouse near the town for the duration and they were all crashing there.

One night, Dez and Igor got into a blazing row. After goading Igor mercilessly, Dez left the situation and went back to the house. Igor arrived several hours later, steaming drunk and mad as hell. He marched straight up to Dez's room, jumped on his bed and began beating several shades of shit out of him while swearing copiously.

Then the light snapped on and Dez entered in his dressing gown, disturbed by the noise. He'd earlier swapped bedrooms with the unfortunate publisher. As you can imagine, that was the end of their project.

There's a slightly duller version of that story involving a British publisher and another version, set in a London Hotel, involving a Belgian publisher but I prefer this one.

I first met Dez Skinn around 1973 when I did a cover for his fanzine, *Fantasy Advertiser*. He went on to work as an editor at IPC and for *Mad* magazine, publish *House of Hammer* and *Starburst* and edit British Marvel Comics before publishing the seminal comic anthology *Warrior*, whose strips, especially *Marvelman*, drawn by Garry Leach, and *V for Vendetta*, drawn by David Lloyd famously brought writer Alan Moore to the attention of American comic publishers. Since the early nineties he's been the publisher and editor of *Comics International*, the monthly UK comic newszine. A controversial character, one of his sayings is "Everything you've heard about me is true".

An argument over ownership of *Warrior* characters and disputed payments led to a well-publicized split between him and Alan Moore, Alan refusing to supply any new material for the magazine except for completing serials he'd already started and breaking off all communication with Dez.

The rumour going around the internet that the split happened because Dez ran off with Alan's wife is a laughable porky, especially if you know *anything* about the personalities involved.

During a Forbidden Planet party one night at UKCAC I was propping up the bar after several pints when Dez ambled over, equally sozzled, and the talk turned to Alan.

"Listen Dez," I ventured, "the British comic industry isn't big enough for this falling out. It needs Alan working in Warrior. You must sort out your differences."

He was nodding sagely at this as Alan arrived in the pub in the company of Karen Berger, who'd just taken him out for dinner, having headhunted him for DC.

"Look," I said to Dez, "there's Alan. Now's your chance! Go over and make it up with him!"

He looked at me, determined.

"By God! You're right! I'll do it!" he said and strode over to Alan, who stopped stock still and stared stonily down at him from his great hairy height.

"Alan," Dez began, "I'm sorry if I've done anything to offend you. We need to continue our work together. Let's put aside our differences. Let's be friends."

Alan regarded him gravely.

"Dez," he rumbled.

"Yes?"

"Fuck off."

It was sometime in the following few months that Alan and Dez both found themselves in attendance at the *CymruCon* science fiction convention in Cardiff. Also there was the self-styled *42nd Squadron*, a gang of mad bastards who were once a common fixture at British SF cons. They were the sort of wackos that always end up being the ones featured in TV news coverage of SF cons, just to demonstrate to the audience how appallingly silly SF fans really are. They'd often disrupt cons with ray gun battles and the like. At one point in the con they started throwing fireworks around inside the hotel and set a wood-panelled wall on fire.

One of their activities was doing a *hit*. Really. For a price, you could take out a contract on anyone attending the con. So Alan decides to take one out on Dez. I believe that it cost him fifty quid, which he thought good value for the money at the time.

The "hit" took place on the Saturday night during the con disco. Dez is bopping on the dance floor, grooving the night away, dancing with the daughter of LionelFanthorpe, who's arguably Britain's worst SF author. He used to write novels to the exact word count he was contracted for, padding them out by an extensive and innovative use of *Roget's Thesaurus*

to repeat the phrase he'd just written several times until it made a whole paragraph.

Suddenly 42nd Squadron strike. In less than ten seconds they have Dez on the floor, whip off his kecks and underpants and throw them to the furthest corner of the disco, spray him with shaving foam, take a polaroid of him, legs akimbo, and vanish, leaving a stunned Dez, blinded by the flash bulb, crawling de-bagged on the floor and wondering what the fuck just hit him.

Copies of the photograph were circulated at a subsequent comic convention in Birmingham to much hilarity and news of the "hit" spread quickly, though Dez had the last laugh when he turned it to his own advantage during a *Warrior* panel. During the Q and A session, a fanzine editor, hoping to embarrass him, stood up and asked him if the alleged incident happened and whether the photo existed.

"Yes!" Dez cried, unabashed, amidst a torrent of laughter and cat calls. "It shows that I'm the only publisher with any balls!"

Another controversial character, part of the UK comics scene in the eighties, was Robbie the Pict. Robbie worked for Ron Turner's *Last Gasp* comic company in the States during the Golden Age of undergrounds and knew the likes of Robert Crumb, Gilbert Shelton, S. Clay Wilson and many others.

Returning to his native Scotland in the late seventies, he rented a room in a Glasgow house that turned out to be the premises of an illegal amphetamine factory and, when it was inevitably busted, he was sent down for a couple of years along with the speed dealers who'd rented him the room. At this time, I was writing and drawing *Brainstorm Comix* and was passed Robbie's prison address by a mutual acquaintance. I started sending him copies of the comics and we began a correspondence that continued after he was released.

Pretty soon he began a wholesale underground comics distribution company called *Planet Wheels* and, once a month, he toured the country in a large blue van – a converted ambulance that housed his stock, a mattress and a wood burning stove–visiting head shops and comic stores to sell his wares. I painted a Planet Wheel*s* logo on one side of the van. *Near Myths* and now DC Thompson artist Graham Manley did the sign on the other side. Robbie would regularly stop the night at our house during his tour and I'd receive the latest batch of imported undergrounds by way of thanks. Some of these, such as *White Whore Funnies* were really outrageous. Pornographic in fact. How the hell was he getting titles such as *Leather Nun* and *Cocaine Comics* into the country?

The other British importer of American UGs, Tony and Carroll

Bennett's long established *Knockabout Comics*, was in continual dispute with UK Customs, who seized their books (very often by Robert Crumb) several times and dragged them through long and expensive court cases. Even though they always won, the legal costs and loss of business due to frozen stock were financially draining, though they did manage to stay in business and are still active today. This is around the time when the Scottish customs were so alert that they impounded a shipment of innocent DC comics bound for AKA in Glagow because they saw that it contained copies of *Wonder Woman* and assumed it was a porno mag.

Robbie, on the other hand, never had one single shipment stopped. How did he do it? How did he manage to outfox Her Majesty's Customs for so long? Simple. All his imports were addressed to "The Scottish Presbyterian Book Society".

He later changed the name of his premises to "The Pictish High Commission" after declaring himself a member of the *Pictish Free State* and refusing to recognize any UK authority. Owing thousands of pounds in unpaid tax, council rates and parking tickets, he disappeared one night and was last heard of living as an outlaw in the Scottish Highlands.

He remains the only person to get Robert Crumb to do a UK signing tour and still owes Knockabout a large amount of cash.

Stories abound concerning Glenn Fabry's many alcohol-fuelled exploits but here I'm going to confine myself to the most oft-repeated ones. Probably best known for his art in *Neverwhere* and his fantastic *Preacher* covers, these days Glenn is much more temperate than in the wild days of his youth, when his legendary drinking bouts led to many a weird, amusing or, indeed, dangerous situation, such as the time he knocked himself out on the UKCAC stage after tripping over the jeans that he'd dropped to moon the audience.

I met Glenn when he was still a teenager pumping gas for a living and contributing to the fanzine *Working Class Superhero* in his spare time and his drawing skill, even then, was prodigious. He had more drawing talent in his little finger than most pros and I happily commissioned him to do a strip for the second issue of *Near Myths* that I edited—the one that was never printed after the publisher did a moonlight flit and left the artwork and all the back issues to be trashed by his landlord, to whom he owed six month's back-rent.

I was instrumental in getting Glenn his first professional work when Pat Mills, with whom I was then working on *Nemesis the Warlock* for 2000AD, needed someone to take Mike McMahon's place as the artist of *Slaine*. I recommended Glenn and he got the gig though, not being used to deadlines, he once had to stay with me for a week in order to finish the job in time. He pencilled the strip on one side of the studio as I inked it on the other.

The most famous Glenn story, that he once, during a dinner DC were having for comic creators in London, bit *Vertigo* editor Karen Berger on the bottom is, unfortunately, not true. He just pretended to.

The second most famous Glenn story is not drink-related. It is this: Before *Preacher* came out, Glenn had a meeting in London with its writer, Garth Ennis to discuss the covers. Afterwards he boarded a train at Victoria for his hometown of Brighton and, finding it to be crowded, had to stand in the corridor next to the locked connecting door at the rear of the train where he started doing a crossword in the *Evening Standard*.

The next thing he knew was being woken up by the bumping of the gurney that was wheeling him down the corridor of a Brighton hospital. He knew it was in Brighton because he could recognize the gold cross atop a local church steeple through a passing window. His arm was broken and the bone of his elbow was jutting horrifyingly through the skin.

What had happened was the apparently not uncommon instance of the back door of the train blowing open when it passes out of a tunnel–something to do with air pressure and something that the train companies like to keep extremely quiet about. Glenn had been discovered, covered in blood, wandering about on the railway line in a state of extreme disorientation.

Some while later, Glenn's back home, his arm in a cast, struggling to meet a deadline when the doorbell goes. The guy looks like a regular copper at first glance but Glenn notices that his badge says he's a member of the Railway Police. He informs Glenn that British Rail is intending to sue him for trespass, for walking around on their rails! The alternative is that Glenn signs a prepared statement. Still a bit woozy after the accident and half-cut on painkillers, Glenn doesn't think it through and signs it to get him off his back. Afterwards he sees that he's signed away all rights to compensation. Sad but true.

Sometimes this following story is set at night in the center of London on a rainy night and sometimes it's a sunny mid-afternoon in the depths of rural England but in essence it goes like this: Glenn's had a drink or two and is strolling along when he hears singing coming from the open door of a church. He's strangely moved to enter and, having done so, takes a pew at the back of the congregation. The vicar takes to the pulpit and begins a sermon so patronising, slimy and sanctimonious that Glenn can stand it no longer. As he staggers up the aisle, the vicar steps back, aghast, and Glenn takes his place at the pulpit, haranguing him and the congregation at their unbridled hypocrisy and the evils of organised religion in general.

Pretty soon two policemen enter and approach him,

"Come on sir," they say, smiling. "Please don't make a scene. Please give it a rest and leave these people to their worship. Come on, we'll take you home."

"Okay," says Glenn, smiling benevolently upon the congregation as he passes down the aisle with the coppers.

Once outside the church, the cops beat the crap out of him and instruct him to bugger off.

As I've indicated previously, the veracity of many of these comic book legends is often suspect, the stories mutating like a virus as they are told and re-told. Through diligent and time-consuming research I have found the previous story to be a complete load of bollocks: the result of Chinese whispers mixed liberally with pure imagination, a perfect example of a story that's evolved in the telling. The aforementioned research involved a quick phone call to Glenn, who was amused to hear it for the first time. He then supplied me with the actual event from which it most probably evolved. Here it is:

Many years ago, teenage Glenn has split up with his girlfriend. He's inconsolable, especially as it's right in the middle of Christmas, and goes to the pub to drown his sorrows.

Emerging a few hours later, he's surprised to be confronted by a near-riot involving rival football fans in Shepperton's Church Square, many of whom have taken the advice "'Tis the season to be jolly" to heart and are falling about blind drunk, bellowing football chants and engaging in random acts of violence. The police were on the scene, indulging in random acts of violence themselves in a futile attempt to restore order.

Bemused, Glenn tried to skirt the surging crowd and escape the chaos, working his way down the side of the square until he found himself hemmed-in before the open door of a church where some sort of Christmas ceremony was taking place inside.

It seemed to Glenn to be a ridiculous situation, something straight out of a comedy movie. Spontaneously, he knocked loudly on the door.

"Let me in!" he shouted, laughing, "I'm a Buddhist!"

Rather than amused by this, the coppers nearby construed it as a criminal act and headed towards him, brandishing their truncheons. Glenn squeezed through the crowd at the side of the church and into the grave-yard, where four coppers chased him around the headstones until he was caught and cuffed. He wasn't beaten up but was taken straight to Kingston prison where he spent the night as a guest of Her Majesty.

Glenn's punishment was compounded by him being banged up in the same cell as two drunken off-duty members of the disreputable *Ulster Defence Regiment* who kept waking him up all night by intermittently chanting "UDR! UDR!"

Next morning he was let off without charge.

––––––––––––

Apocryphal stories about Glenn abound. One is that he was hit by an ambulance whilst crossing the road and died in the vehicle as it was rushing him to hospital. He heard this from a fanboy who nearly fainted upon seeing him, believing him to be many months dead.

One time, Glenn gets a lift to a *Deadline* party in a mini crammed with artificial legs from a writer who also works at a hospital. At the pub it turns out that this guy is also a faith healer and offers to sort out any problems he might have.

Joking, Glenn says "Well, you can try it on my liver."

The writer places his hands on the back of Glenn, who has the disconcerting sensation of them going deep inside his body and farting about with his innards. He removes his hands and tells Glenn that his liver's fine.

After a full night's drinking, by one in the morning Glenn's ended up back at the *Deadline* office in the company of Garry Leach, Will Simpson, who's lying on his back and drunkenly performing a rendition of *Riders on the Storm* to no one in particular, and editor Dave Elliot who brings out the only alcohol he has there: a particularly potent Jamaican rum in a green bottle that seems to Glenn to be pulsing with light…

Glenn wakes up at six o'clock in the morning, in his bare feet, forty miles away on a platform at Sunbury railway station. How he got there is a total mystery. His shoes were still in the office.

––––––––––––

On another occasion, drinking in a London pub with *Hellblazer* and *Preacher* artist Steve Dillon, the conversation turned to drawing styles. Scott McCloud claims to have invented the *twenty-four hour comic* but Steve was doing them long before–and professionally, not just as exercises in self-expression. Using his very effective storytelling technique,

Steve would draw a twenty-four page comic taking, on an average of six panels per page, five minutes per panel for pencils and five minutes per panel for inks–an hour per page. He'd sit down and do the whole book in one sitting. Admittedly he didn't write or letter them but his comics were of a totally professional standard and a joy to read, unlike most of the hastily scribbled and eminently forgettable examples of twenty-four hour comics that I've ever come across.

Steve, who began drawing comics professionally at the age of six-teen, told Glenn that at that age he spent much more time on his drawings, doing really detailed work. This sparked a debate between them, Glenn trying to persuade him to leave his straightforward, fast-paced style and have a try at going back to detailed illustration.

At some point late in the night, Glenn disappeared and Steve went to the loo, where he found him being sick in the toilet. Glenn spots him and carries on the conversation.

"No, no Steve…" Glenn slurs in between pukes, "…I mean it." BARF! "Spend more time on your…" BARF! "…drawing so you can be…" BARF! "…just like me."

When I spoke to Glenn about the stories concerning him in this book, the latter was his favourite. The version that Garth Ennis tells is different, ending with Glenn saying "If only you'd put in the effort, you'd be where I am now!" before falling into the urinal.

It took Steve Dillon several years to evolve his fast and fluid style, the result of a prolific output and constant deadline pressures. Early on in his career, he'd completed an episode of *Judge Dredd*, lettered by 2000AD mainstay Tom Frame, and they went for a well-earned pint or two in their local boozer on a Thursday afternoon. The strip had to be delivered on the Friday so it could go to print first thing the following Monday morning. They'd come from Steve's studio, the artwork in his portfolio, so he could take it straight to the 2000AD offices next day.

Later that night, upon arriving home, it suddenly occurred to Steve that something was missing.

"Oh shit!" thought Steve. "I've left the portfolio on the bus!"

Next morning he went straight to the bus depot, hoping that it had been handed in at the lost property office. It hadn't.

At IPC's King's Reach Tower, editor Steve McManus hit the roof. Dredd was the comic's flagship strip and the missing episode left a sickening void in the middle of the next issue.

"Don't worry," promised Dillon, "I'll get it here by Monday morning. I guarantee."

Steve hared back to his studio and, with Tom Frame lettering, ruling panel borders and filling in blacks on one side of the room and him drawing it on the other, they worked non-stop, night and day for the entire weekend, until the whole seven-page strip was recreated by early Monday morning.

They duly delivered it, as promised, and it went off to the printer on time, along with the rest of the issue. Steve McManus was extremely impressed and congratulated Steve and Tom on their professionalism.

Right: after that, they *really* deserved a well-earned pint and returned to their local to relax. They were greeted by the publican.

"Oh, Steve," he said, pulling their pints, "Is this your portfolio? Somebody left it in the bar on Thursday night."

Steve is another legendary drinker though, unlike Glenn, nobody ever seems to have seen him drunk. At conventions he always used to pride himself on being the last one to leave the bar–the last man standing. As I've related, the bar at the *UK Comic Art Convention* pro hotel often used to serve as long as there were hotel guests in it. The latest I remember leaving it was seven-thirty in the morning and there was still a good two dozen people there, including Steve, Heidi McDonald, Garth Ennis, Si Spencer and his partner Colleen who were doing their musical thang.

Si wrote comics, including *Books of Magic*, and edited *Deadline* for several years before becoming a TV scriptwriter, notably on *Eastenders*. He's currently writing episodes of the *Dr Who* spin-off series *Torchwood*. He and Colleen, who were well-known regulars in Brit comic convention pro bars, had the nickname *The Human Jukebox*. You could ask for literally any song and they'd sing it. I've never seen them stumped. They wouldn't only know all the lyrics but one of them would sing the backing vocals. At the particular session mentioned above they did requests as varied as *The Streets of Laredo* for Garth Ennis and *Every Sperm is Sacred* from *Monty Python's Meaning of Life* for me.

Singing isn't in this next story at all but I need a tenuous link, so that'll do. In 2005, *Marvelman* artist Garry Leach was over in Northern Ireland to take a comic class, part of *the Belfast Cathedral Arts Festival*, with *Judge Dredd* artist Rufus Dayglo and Will Simpson, who had an exhibition of his artwork as part of the event. The private view was held on the top floor of a half-deserted manky old building the council had only recently acquired.

The free drinks are flowing like the crystal streams of heaven when Garry, who's been eyeing up a couple of young women who've taken his fancy, realises that, after all the beer, what he really needs to do is take an urgent leak. He asks Will where the loo is but discovers that there is none. The only bit of the building that's functional is the exhibition area, especially decorated in time for the event.

By this point, he's absolutely bursting. Will tells him that there's a pub just down the street and he should go and use their toilet but Garry is really desperate. Picking up his empty pint glass, he heads off down the stairs. You can see where I'm going with this one, can't you?

Meanwhile, the two colleens are talking to Will. They're really into manga and want to know how you go about publishing a comic. Will tells them they should really speak to Garry: he published the *A1* comic anthology in the 90s and is planning to do so again.

"He's just gone for a waz." says Will. "He'll be back in a few minutes".

Wanting to make sure they don't miss Garry, the girls head on down the stairs, hoping to meet him on the way back

Reaching the ground floor corridor, they spot Garry, who's in the space under the steps and is, unseen by them, relieving himself into his beer glass.

"Mr Leach?"

Garry's horrified. He can't stop peeing but these girls are getting closer and asking him all sorts of questions. He's carrying on the conversation over his shoulder, his body in the shadow of the stairs, gamely trying to answer them and glancing down in panic as the level of urine fast approaches the top of the glass. Gritting his teeth, he manages to put his bladder on hold just as the pee reaches the top of the glass. It's barely held in check by surface tension as he slowly turns around to face the girls, his wedding tackle still hanging out but mercifully hidden by his large loose shirt.

"What on earth are you doing down there, Garry?"

It's Sarah, the festival organiser, coming down the stairs.

"Are you alright?"

"I'm, er, just looking for some music." he adlibs, indicating the empty filing cabinet and two plastic trash bags under the steps.

Not a very convincing answer but she left it at that. They all returned to the exhibition where Garry rid himself of the pint of pee at the first opportunity, though he did consider giving it to *Hellboy* and *Aliens vs Predator* screenwriter Pete Briggs, who had allegedly spent that evening making himself about as popular as a fart in an aromatherapy class.

When Garry was a young up-and-coming artist, working for 2000AD, he arrived one day at King's Reach Tower to deliver some finished artwork. The tower block housed all of the IPC empire's offices, publishing everything from women's magazines to newspapers. Passing through the "Juvenile Floor" dedicated to their various comic and teen mag titles, he was stopped by the editor of *My Guy* magazine, a publication aimed at the teenage girls' romance market, who urgently needed to fill in a space in the "pen pals" section. All she needed was a photo and address. Garry reluctantly agreed after being assured that he needn't answer any correspondence he may be sent, had his picture taken and promptly forgot about it.

Around eight weeks later, Garry starts to receive letters from teenage girls from all over the world. The IPC mags and comics were distributed throughout the British Commonwealth, from Canada to Kenya and he got the lot.

Notable was one accompanied by a photo of an attractive young lady from the north of England.

The letter read "Hi, I'm seventeen and very sexy. I have big breasts. Please phone me up and we'll get together and have great sex."

Garry ignored it, along with the rest, and, again, forgot about it.

Two weeks later, he meets up with John Higgins and some other 2000AD regulars for a beer.

"Here, look at this," he says, producing a small package. Carefully unwrapping it, he shows the others. Inside is a small sandwich: two slices of bread wrapped around a turd.

The accompanying letter rationalized the contents:

"You fucker. If you can't even be bothered phoning me up, eat shit and die."

————————

At a con in the eighties in Birmingham, *Doctor Strange* artist Frank Brunner was on a panel discussion before an audience several hundred strong. In the Q and A session, a fan asked him what the greatest influence was on his work. Without hesitation, he grabbed the mike and said "Drugs."

It got a great laugh but there is more than a grain of truth in his answer. In my experience, quite a few comic writers and artists have produced their best work while stoned. In fact, many of these are stoned most of the time, so this is no great coincidence.

One *Hellblazer* writer was receiving his weekly delivery of dope when his dealer asked him if he wanted some free magic mushrooms. Apparently she'd been lumbered with tons of the stuff and wanted to get it off her hands. She left him two large bags' full, leaving him to ponder exactly how to store the mushrooms: if he left them alone they'd go mouldy and he hadn't the means to dry them all out. He decided to boil them all up in water and store the juice in the fridge.

Having filled every suitable container, from milk bottles to jam jars, he found that a quantity of the concentrated liquid still remained in the pan so decided to make himself a cup of coffee with it.

Getting back to work, he took his place at his desk and slowly sipped the coffee while contemplating the story he was about to type up.

He came to with a start. He'd been sitting in the same spot, staring at the wall for forty-eight hours.

I met Mike Netzer at the Alicante Festival in 2004, after being in his company on the comic pro email discussion group *Panel2Panel* for a few years. With his long flowing grey hair and voluminous beard, he looked like Moses, a likeness reinforced by the wooden staff he carried.

Mike burst onto the comic scene in the 1970s and drew many mainstream superhero comics, including *Superman, Batman, Spider-Man*, and *Wonder Woman* until having a spiritual awakening and moving to Israel. He now believes he's the second coming and the longer you talk with him, the more you will too. Search and find his website, read his controversial and well thought-out ideas and decide for yourself whether he's the new messiah or as mad as a box of frogs.

One night over a few beers he recounted how, in 1979, he had been working on a Spiderman comic for Marvel, on assignment from Neal Adams' *Continuity Studios* in New York when editor Jim Shooter asked him to produce a cover for a new title, *Rom the Robot* (Later titled *Rom the Space Knight*). Shooter wanted a striking and violent image, the robot terrorizing some exotic tribal villagers.

Try as he might, Mike had reached a mental stage where he couldn't bear to depict violence in his artwork any more. For the past couple of years he'd been developing a philosophy, a new religion designed to bring peace to America. Mike thinks big. He stayed up all night and, in the morning, took the finished cover to the Marvel offices— an illustration of a messiah robot blessing his devoted villagers. At this point the story hadn't even been written but it wasn't what Shooter wanted and he sent Mike away with a flea in his ear to redraw it.

So he returns to Continuity and, instead of working on the cover, he paints a picture of Superman. The first Christopher Reeves movie had only recently been released, so he bases the character on him. For some strange reason he adds a phantom horse in the background. Over a decade later, Reeves is paralyzed after falling from one.

Next day he arrives early at Marvel, intending to return the cover and argue its merits but Shooter hasn't arrived yet. As he waits, he slowly realizes that there's no way the "Benevolent Rom" robot artwork will be accepted. Coming to a life-changing decision, he rips it up, puts the pieces in an envelope along with a note that basically says "I quit" and leaves it for Shooter. Mike then spends the day in Central Park where, at some point, he decides to drop a tab of acid.

He gets back to Continuity later in the day, zonked out of his skull. His boss and mentor, Neal Adams, totally freaks. This is the last straw. Apparently Mike's been spending most of his time in the studio doing religious drawings and making hundreds of copies on the company's photocopier, and now he's cocked up the cover assignment. Adams gives him one last chance–a piece of movie storyboarding needs finishing to meet the deadline next morning. He leaves Mike alone in the studio and goes home for the night.

Despite the acid Mike finishes the work, by which time his drastically altered consciousness has dreamt up a grand scheme to go immediately to Detroit and begin a countrywide comic-fuelled evangelical crusade. Seems reasonable to me.

So, at three in the morning, he locks up the studio and heads off down the street, stony broke and bound for Detroit. Hailing a cab, he asks to be taken to the airport where he gets out and walks to the terminal. The driver runs after him, demanding his money. Mike tells him he simply asked if he'd take him to the airport. He didn't say he'd pay. Anyhow, he's got no money, so he can't. Astonishingly, the cabbie gives it up as a bad job and gives Mike his card, asking him to pay when he can.

Mike wanders through the mostly deserted terminal till he sees a corridor signposted as being off-limits to the public. Lifting the barrier, he goes straight on in there and finds himself passing dreamlike through a maze of empty corridors and unlit offices till he opens a door and enters a large, garish, florescent-lit staff cafeteria, where airport workers are sitting around drinking coffee and arguing about football games. Nobody pays a blind bit of notice to the spaced-out prophet ambling through their midst. "Lo! He walked among them and they knew him not."

Emerging from the cafeteria exit, he's now in a massive hanger, the open runway visible at the other end. Between him and it stands a jet plane, its lights on and a stair leading up to the tail door. Up he goes, into the plane and down the aisle, stepping over the vacuum cleaner of the guy cleaning the plane, who carries on as if nothing's happened. Arriving in the cockpit, Mike plonks himself down in the captain's seat and starts dicking around with the levers and switches.

About half an hour later a security guy appears and politely invites him to leave the plane. On the tarmac, two cops are waiting for him but, after a lengthy grilling by the airport manager, they decide he's harmless and take him to a general hospital, where they leave him for psychiatric evaluation as he slowly comes down off his trip. After a phone call by the psychiatrist to Neal Adams to confirm Mike's who he says he is, he's let off with a caution and told to bugger off.

By the time he gets back to Continuity, Neal Adams has arranged a bus ticket for him to Detroit. And a letter from Jim Shooter has arrived-offering him a raise if he'll do more work for Marvel!

I think the most amazing thing about this hijack story is not Mike's sheer audacity nor the ease with which he gained access to the restricted areas of the airport but how things have changed politically so much since then. These days he'd be locked up without trial and the keys thrown down the nearest sewer. Of course, a New York cab driver will still graciously allow you to pay when you can afford to.

This next one may quite well be approaching the truth as Grant has told it to just about everybody who would stop and listen.

After making his name in America and a small fortune with titles such as *Animal Man*, *Doom Patrol* and *Arkham Asylum* in his first stint with DC, Grant Morrison shaved his head, took a whole year off and travelled the world till his money ran out.

Packing his bag one sunny morning in a hotel room in Thailand and about to leave for India, he was presented with a dilemma: what should he do with his stash? He was loath to flush away the small collection of drugs he'd accumulated and equally loath to attempt to smuggle them through Indian customs, so he took the third path. He gobbed the lot. The type and quantity of these drugs change, depending on who's telling the story, but they're along these lines: a joint's worth of thai grass, a lump of opiated hash, a tab of acid and a couple of Es. Bouyed up by this admirable application of the "waste not, want not" principle, he checked out and caught a taxi to the airport.

The flight, although uneventful from his fellow passengers' point of view, was a delirious phantasmagoria from that of Grant who was, by now, either a total mess or in an ecstatic state bordering on godhood, depending upon your criteria.

As the plane began its descent to Bombay, his hallucinogenic reverie was suddenly shattered as the narcotic cocktail he'd taken for breakfast began to have a drastic and unnerving effect upon his digestive system. His guts churned and, enhanced by the acid, his belly became uncomfortably distended as grumbling pockets of trapped wind battled it out for supremacy. In his hammered state, it took him a few minutes to read his body signals but he eventually realised what he had to do. He needed to fart. Urgently. It was fast building into a peristaltic tsunami with

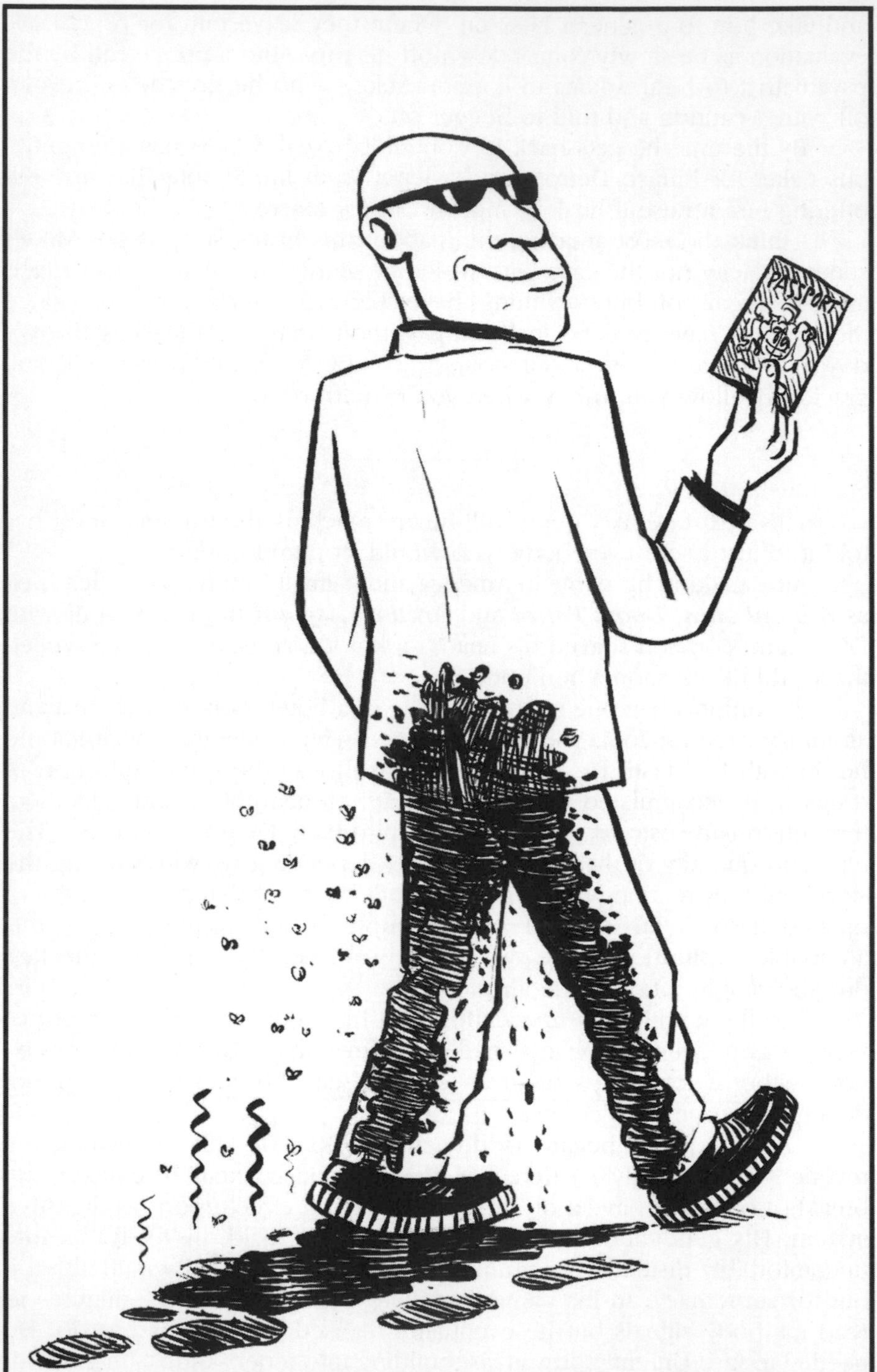
PASSPORT

a disturbingly high decibel potential.

He felt too embarrassed to simply let rip. The flight was crowded. They'd all hear his backdoor trumpet and laugh at him. It would scar him for life: their mocking faces appearing in black and white flashback whenever he needed to act cool.

He considered the toilet: it wasn't an option. He'd never reach it in time. Trapped in his window seat with two huge Indian matriarchs wedged in the seats between him and the aisle, his rectum ballooned with expanding gas, threatening to imminently explode.

In the hope of passing a silent one, he mentally chanted a tantric mantra and concentrated. Using preternatural skill, he carefully and very slowly began to dilate his sphincter, his buttocks spasming mightily as he fought to keep the tremendous flatulent pressures finely balanced. He was rewarded by a slow, controlled, silent emission that seemed to take forever.

Eventually he was completely deflated, sinking contentedly back into his chair in the delight of sheer relief. Several heads turned at the smell but–hey! It could have been anyone!

Still spaced out, arriving at Bombay airport he strode confidently up to the customs in his elegant white linen suit, suddenly feeling like the archetypical Englishman abroad. The fact that Grant is Scottish didn't mar this whimsical fancy. The customs officers quickly and unaccountably waved him through and he proceeded straight to his hotel. In his room, he immediately headed for the full-length mirror to appreciate what a fine figure he cut: the intrepid traveller, the sophisticated and handsomely cynical hero of a thousand adventures.

Then he noticed the stain. Turning around and looking back he saw that his white suit was soaked in dark brown from his waist to his shoes.

There's a variant of the above with Hong Kong as the destination.

―――――――

With *X-Men* writer Pete Milligan, Grant and his girlfriend attended the wedding of *Tank Girl* and *Gorillaz* artist Jamie Hewlett in Brighton. Killing time before the ceremony, the three of them took a stroll along the famous beach, throwing pebbles into the sea. Coming across a knackered old boat, they decided to use it for target practice, rattling its side with stones. They stopped abruptly, however, when a large and quite furious fisherman rose up from the other side of his cherished boat, cursing them loudly and threatening them with imediate and sickeningly violent retribution. They quickly turned to walk away only to be confronted by two more fishermen of a similar demeanour rolling up their sleeves and striding towards them, fists clenched.

"Stay back!" warned Grant, making slicing motions with his hand. "I know karate!"

Grant and Pete later attended the wedding, their suits torn and muddied and their faces heavily bruised.

In the late 90s, Grant and *Hellbalzer* and *2020 Visions* writer Jamie Delano are guests at a convention in Stockholm. They're met at the airport by their con minders, taken to their hotel to drop off their bags and taken out for dinner. Being vegetarians the pair both have trouble with the menu, which seems to offer nothing but meat and dried salted fish, and they eat very little.

Gin and tonic is Jamie's tipple of choice, a drink he usually sips at convention bars until the small hours with no discernable effect on his urbane and soft-spoken manner. This restaurant doesn't do G&Ts so his hosts suggest schnapps instead. Jamie's heard of schnapps of course but has never tried it before and his curiosity gets the better of him. So they buy him a bottle. That's right: a whole bottle of a drink that's so pernicious it can strip paint. Unfortunately, Jamie discovers that he has a taste for it.

Four hours later at the con disco, Jamie is totally rat-arsed. At about one in the morning, he suddenly stands up, slurs to Grant that he's going to the loo and weaves his way unsteadily across the dance floor in its general direction.

Half an hour later he hasn't returned so Grant tells the minders that he's going to have a look. He enters the toilet but can't see anyone.

"Jamie?"

There's no response but the toilet isn't completely deserted–he sees that there's someone in one of the cubicles, shoes and trousers visible beneath the stall door.

"Jamie? Are you in there?"

An affirmative groan comes from inside. Grant finds that the door is unlocked and he gently pushes it open.

Jamie is slumped on the toilet, his pants around his ankles. Opening his eyes with great difficulty, he sees Grant.

"For Christ's sake get me back to the hotel."

"Okay," says Grant. "Can you stand up?"

His head spinning, Jamie tries to move, provoking an immediate and spectacular reaction. Lurching forward he gives a mighty heave and retches the contents of his stomach into his underpants.

Luckily for Grant, at this point their minders turn up and, assessing the situation, heroically scoop out the contents of Jamie's briefs with paper towels. Throwing up has worked wonders and Jamie starts to snap out of it. They manage to get his trousers back up and support him as he staggers back into the disco.

Halfway across the dance floor he stops and points at the assembled conventioneers.

"You fucking Swedish bastards!" he shouts. " You've fucking poisoned me, you fucking wankers!"

The minders have to struggle to drag him across the dance floor, through the posh lobby and out of the hotel, all the while Jamie hurling abuse at Swedes and Sweden in general in the most colourful terms you can imagine.

They bundle Jamie into a taxi. Grant, following him in, turns to their hosts and apologizes for Jamie's outburst.

"No, that was great!" says one laughing. "We understand the British sense of humour!"

Apparently, at exactly the same time that Jamie was incapacitated, back in Britain his Grandad died. Jamie reckoned that the old bastard was trying to take him with him.

The late Archie Goodwin, writer and editor, was one of the nicest men in comics. Always even-tempered and polite, it's really hard to imagine him getting into a blind fury. But one time he did. Married and living in New York and with a new baby, he and Anne were constantly having their sleep disturbed by the car alarm of a neighbour. It was one of the motion detector type–the sort that goes off if someone breaks wind three blocks away.

Archie and the rest of the neighbours complained continually to the owner, an obnoxious yuppie who simply replied by being abusive.

One night was the final straw for the sleep deprived Archie when he was awakened for the fifth time in two hours by the alarm. He snapped. Grabbing a recently filled diaper from the trash, he ran downstairs into the street and smeared its contents all over the car's windscreen.

And if you don't believe it, Archie told me that one.

Archie died in 1998, following an eight-year battle with cancer, undergoing chemotherapy followed by what seemed to be a full recovery several times. Shortly after his first bout of chemo, he returned to work and attended a comic retailer's conference in Hawaii. Naturally, his colleagues were very sensitive to his condition and were very concerned to make sure he was okay.

So, Archie decides to go for a stroll and several follow him at a discrete distance. Arriving at the top of a cliff, he walks right up to the edge to take in the impressive panorama. His minders are a little unnerved.

"Hey, Archie, be careful!" one calls out.

A little pissed off at being treated with kid gloves, he decides to wind them up. Looking down, he sees there's a ledge a few feet below him and, without any more ado, leaps out of their sight down onto it. Except that it's not a ledge. It's just a bunch of grass growing out from the cliff face. He passes straight through it and plummets two hundred feet to land, fortunately, in the Pacific.

I like to imagine that he looked a little like James Bond as he walked ashore, out of the surf, in his dripping wet business suit.

───────

Simon Bisley's an extremely talented artist who's had a stint as a wrestler and is the drummer in a heavy metal band, *Bloodhammer*. Tall, heavily muscled and tattooed, he can appear a little formidable but I've always found him cool and friendly. Simon was one of the first megastar comic artists, with a huge fan base and a rock star aura. He first shot to fame drawing *Slaine,* written by Pat Mills, in *2000AD*, though his first professional strip, in the same publication, was *ABC Warriors*, also written by Pat. Previously, the Warriors had been illustrated by myself in Pat's *Nemesis the Warlock*, so Simon had to follow on from my designs of the robot anti-heroes, the reason, I think, why the first few times I met him he always called me "Guv'nor". Simon's rock star manner and wicked sense of humour have generated quite few comic book urban legends, the following being my favourites.

Simon drew *Judgement on Gotham*, the first Batman/Judge Dredd team-up and, when it was published in 1991, he did a signing with writers John Wagner and Alan Grant at the Virgin Megastore in London's Oxford Street. It was a massive event. They pulled around four thousand punters. They drew a bigger crowd than those of David Bowie and Elton John's then-recent signings at the same venue combined. The queue was four deep, went around the block and the London Constabulary made it abundantly clear to the Megastore that they weren't too happy about this horde of comic freaks cluttering up their nice pavements and could they get shut of them as soon as possible?

At signings, you always get some fans who arrive bearing carrier bags full of everything you've ever had in print so the store made a condition—only one item signed per customer and that had to be *Judgement on Gotham*, bought on the premises.

To move the punters through as fast as possible, John, Alan and Simon form a production line. Copies arrive before John, are passed to Alan and then to Simon at mind numbing speed. All the way through this, Simon isn't even looking at the line. He's chatting to an attractive young lady who's crouching by his side. After an hour or so of this, a copy is pushed before John who quickly scribbles his name on it.

Before he can pass it on a weedy voice pipes up, "Hey, *you!*"

John looks up wearily at a twelve year old nerd, accompanied by his father. Dad says nothing throughout this but his face is drawn and resigned. The poor bastard's been waiting in line for five hours.

"Don't just sign it!" the lad continues. "Put *To Mathew* first."

Big John doesn't usually take any lip but the line is still disappearing over the horizon, so he adds "To Mathew" with his gold felt-tip pen and slings it to Alan. Alan (who told me this story) grabs the book and adds his moniker beneath John's. A finger prods his arm.

"Hey, *you!*" the snotty kid shouts. " I just told *him!* Don't just sign it, put *To Mathew* first!"

Likewise, Alan, a feisty Glaswegian, doesn't usually take any shit but takes a deep breath and dedicates (or, "personalizes" if you're an American) the book "To Mathew" and passes it to the Biz.

Still focussed on his miniskirted companion, Simon is autographing the thing when the kid jabs his frighteningly brawny arm.

"*You!*" he practically screams. "I just told them two! Don't just sign it! Put *To Mathew* first!"

Simon slowly turns around, looks up and takes him in at a glance. Without pausing, he takes his big gold pen, scrawls the dedication, claps the book shut, hands it back and continues his conversation while Mathew, his father in tow, exits stage right.

What Mathew couldn't see and what Alan could was that Simon had written "Fuck off Mathew!" in nice big caps all over the first page.

There's a story that Simon, on receiving a huge check for *Judgement on Gotham* immediately ran out and bought a Porsche. Within twenty minutes he allegedly wrapped it up on an intersection. The car was a total write-off. Simon was fine.

Another signing story: Simon's at the San Diego Comicon, doing a session for a long line of fans. The next punter in line produces an Image comic he's just bought for forty dollars, carefully extricates it from its mylar bag and gingerly places it on the table before the Biz.

"Could you please sign the cover?" he asks.

"Sure, mate." says Simon and raises his pen, then stops. Puzzled, he studies the cover, opens the comic and has a quick flip through the pages before handing it back.

"Sorry, mate," he says. "I can't sign this. I don't have any work in it."

Undeterred, the fanboy puts it back on the table.

"I know you haven't but can you please sign it for me anyway?" he persists.

"No, I can't. I never sign any work that I've not done. I just don't do it, okay?" says Simon and hands it over again.

The guy, now annoyed, returns it to the table.

"Look, just sign it for me, won't you?" he whines. "Just do it!"

Simon looks down at the comic then, taking it in both hands, he scrunches it up, rolling into a tight tube and grasps it in his left hand. His right hand reaches up, grabs the guy by lapel and yanks him down so that the terrified punter is nose-to-nose with the seemingly furious Biz.

Gesturing with the rolled-up comic, Simon growls "Look–if you don't piss off I'm going to stick this right up your arse."

A couple of seconds pass as the guy's face freezes in an attitude of horror.

Simon lets go of his lapel and smiles serenely as the fan straightens up and backs off, shaking. Placing it on the table, Simon slowly unrolls the crumpled comic and hands it back to him.

"Only joking!" he says cheerfully.

The guy didn't ask again.

Liam Sharpe, X-Men artist and *Mam Tor* publisher, told me this one. In San Diego, he and Simon are strolling over from the convention center to ***Dick's Last Resort*** for a beer. Dick's is where most Brit artists usually end up, mainly because the beer's good, it stays open till two in the morning and you can sit outside in the courtyard and smoke. The staff are also quite amusing as they get hired for their bad attitude and wear tee-shirts bearing legends such as "Dick U" or "I don't know jack but I know Dick" or "Everyone's got a little bit of Dick in them" and so forth.

So, they're walking down the sidewalk and they pass a young couple walking in the opposite direction. The woman smiles at Simon, who can't help but notice her large but perfectly formed breasts through her flimsy blouse.

"Hi!" says Simon. "How are you doing?"

"Just fine," she replies, laughing. She seems like a fun girl.

Simon pulls a wad of notes out of his pocket and peels off a fifty dollar bill.

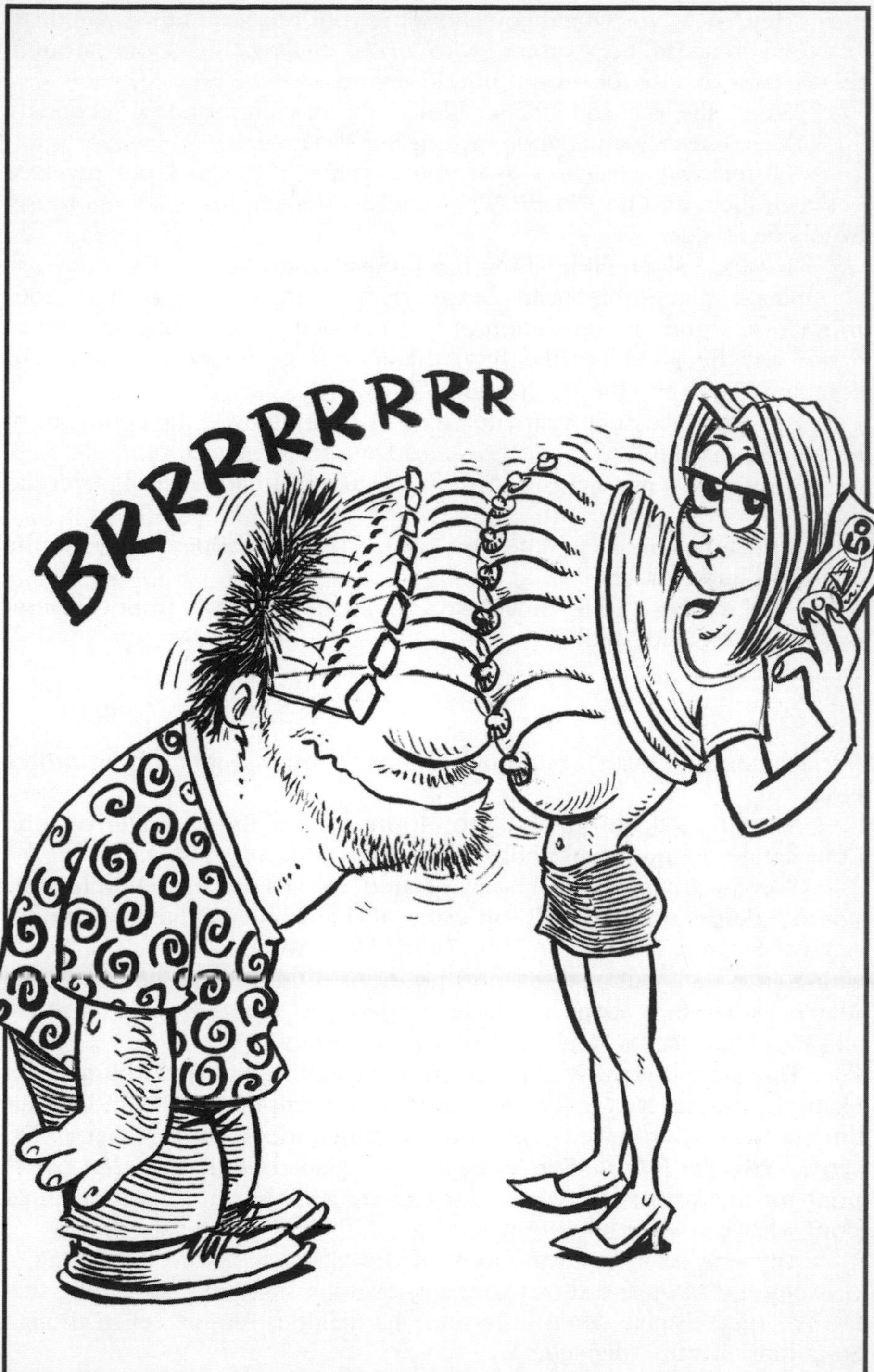
BRRRRRRRR
50

"Hey," he says, "would you show me your breasts if I give you this?"

She looks at her partner, who nods, smiling. She looks around: there's nobody else for several hundred yards.

"Sure!" she says and lifts her blouse to her chin for a few seconds.

"Well, cheers!" says Simon, giving her the note.

"I'll tell you what. If I give you another fifty, can I put my face between them and go *BRRRRR*?" he adds, shaking his head vigorously from side to side.

"I guess," she replies, lifting her blouse again.

Simon places his head between her ample hooters and goes *BRRRRR!* Upon his completion of this manoeuvre, she pulls her blouse down and he gives her the fifty, thanks her profusely and they part company, Liam and the Biz heading off to Dick's.

A night exactly one year later, they're both sitting in the courtyard of Dick's at a table full of comic pros and Liam relates the story.

"Hey, wait a minute!" says Simon. "That never happened. I never did that!"

Just at this moment, the very same couple happen to enter the courtyard and spot Simon.

"Well, hi there!" the woman says, pulls up her top in front of everyone and goes "BRRRRRR!"

———————

I'll conclude with a little mystery that doesn't seem to fit anywhere else.

As you no doubt know, Alan Moore created the character of John Constantine during his groundbreaking run on *Swamp Thing*.

There's an apocryphal story, stated as fact in the encyclopedic *Comics Between the Panels* by Mike Richardson and Steve Duin, of original Swamp Thing writer Len Wein, Marv Wolfman, and Paul Levitz sitting in a café during a San Diego *ComicCon* despondently reading Alan's first Swampy script. The faces of these top writers are ashen as they all realize that they'd suddenly become dinosaurs.

This story is actually a load of unmitigated tripe. Marv Wolfman, for example, has never ever seen a Swamp Thing script in his life and, at this time, was already a huge fan of Alan's writing through *Warrior*. Marv's DC series *Crisis On Infinite Earths*, begun two years later, hasn't been out of print for the last twenty years. Not exactly a dinosaur. I won't put into print what Len Wein told me when I asked him about the anecdote.

Anyhow, Alan based the look of the chain-smoking Constantine, a cockney *wide boy* and urban sorcerer, on rock star Sting–something that DC has tried to play down ever since for litigious reasons, even though Sting himself was delighted.

One day during his stint on *Swamp Thing*, Alan's sitting in a London Café, when he happens to look up and sees John Constantine himself walking through the door, large as life. This guy *is* Constantine; looks like Sting, cigarette in his mouth, light brown trenchcoat, the works. As he passes by Alan's table, he looks down at him, winks and walks out of sight around a corner. Alan sits there gobsmacked. No, he doesn't want to go and verify what he saw. That way lies madness. He finishes his coffee and leaves.

A couple of years later, Constantine gets his own title, *Hellblazer*, written by Jamie Delano. One day Jamie's walking up the steps to the British Museum in London, on his way to do some research. To his utter astonishment, as he reaches the top, Constantine-perhaps the same guy Alan saw-walks out of the museum, lights up a fag*, looks at him, winks and walks off, leaving Jamie staring after him in disbelief.

British slang for "cigarette".
The first time that Martin Skidmore, editor and publisher of the UK comics fanzine Fantasy Unlimited *was in New York, staying in a sleazy downtown dump, he ran out of ciggies in the middle of the night. He went out of the hotel, approached what amounted to a street gang and asked "Hey, guys. Do you know where I can find some fags?" He barely escaped with his life.* •

ABOUT THE AUTHOR

BRYAN TALBOT

Bryan Talbot has written and drawn underground and alternative comics, notably *Brainstorm!,* UK and American science fiction and superhero stories such as *Judge Dredd, Nemesis the Warlock, Teknophage, The Nazz* and *Legends of the Dark Knight,* DC Vertigo titles including *Hellblazer, Sandman, The Dreaming* and *Fables* and the graphic novels for which he is best known: *The Adventures of Luther Arkwright, Heart of Empire, The Tale of One Bad Rat* and *Alice in Sunderland.* He is currently writing the supernatural comedy

miniseries *Cherubs!* for Desperado, drawn by Mark Stafford, and writing and drawing a new steampunk graphic novel, *Grandville.* Later this year, NBM is publishing *The Art of Bryan Talbot,* collecting together for the first time many of his book and magazine illustrations. •

During the hectic Heart of Empire two-week tour of Italy, Talbot relaxes back at the hotel by soaking his feet in the bidet.

WWW.BRYAN-TALBOT.COM

ABOUT THE ARTIST

HUNT EMERSON

Hunt Emerson. Born Newcastle 1952; currently lives in Birmingham, UK. Has been a cartoonist since the early 1970s, and has published around 25 books of his iconoclastic comic strips, including *The Cartoon Lady Chatterley's Lover, The Rime of the Ancient Mariner,* and *Casanova's Last Stand.* His characters include Firkin the Cat, (a strip of sexual satire that has run in Fiesta magazine, UK , since 1981) Calculus Cat, (the cat that hates television), PussPuss, (yes - another cat!), Max Zillion and Alto Ego, (a jazz musician and his saxophone), Alan Rabbit, and many more. His comic books have been translated into a dozen languages. In 2000 he was chosen for inclusion in the exhibition "Les Maitres de la Bande Dessinee Europeenne" by the Bibliotheque Nationale de France and the CNBDI, Angouleme. •

WWW.LARGECOW.DEMON.CO.UK

The King and I:
Bryan Talbot and Jack Kirby,
San Diego Comicon 1989

ON SALE NOW!

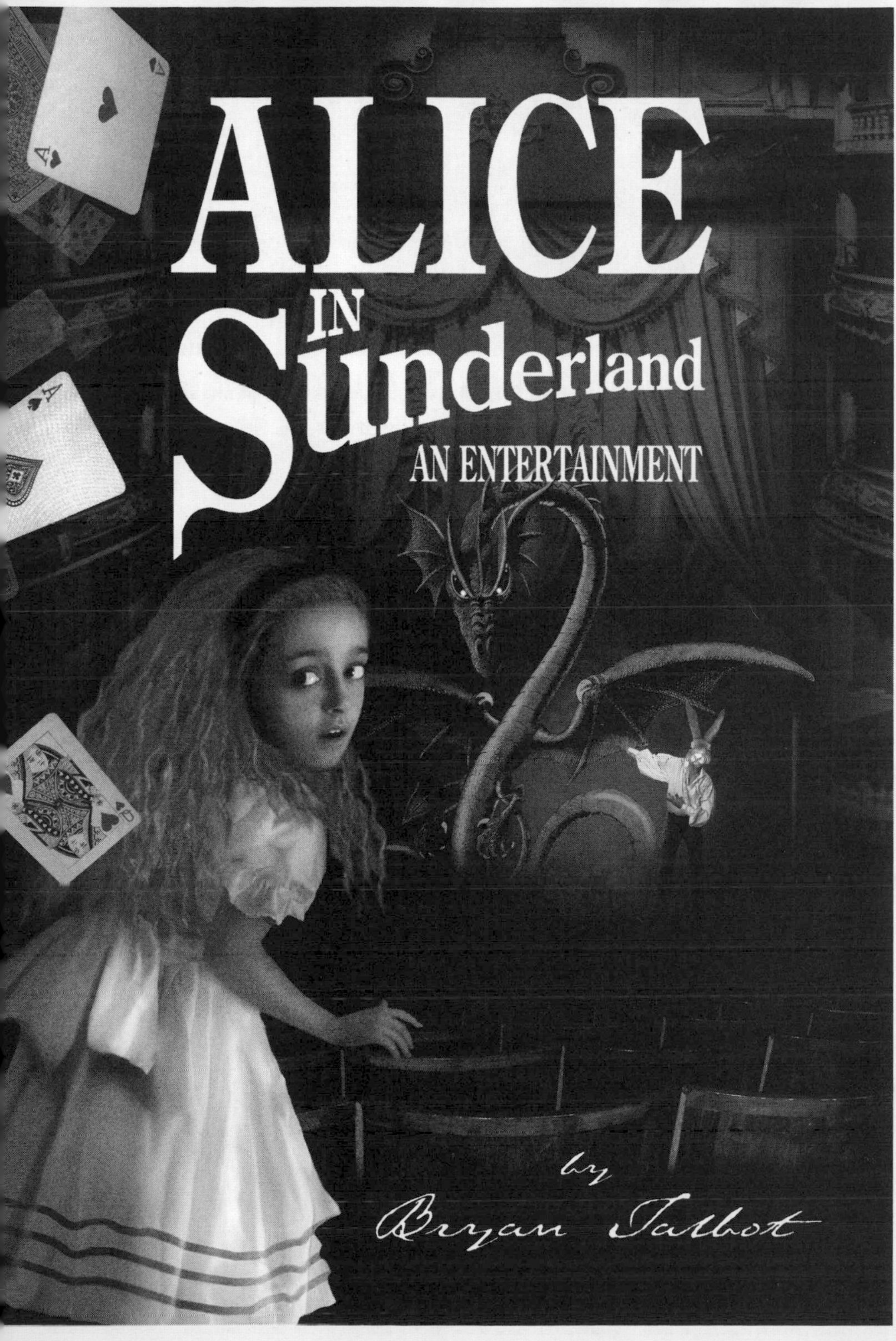
ALICE
IN
Sunderland
AN ENTERTAINMENT
by
Bryan Talbot

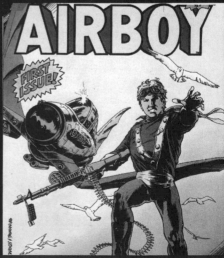